Strong One

GODLY WISDOM FOR THE PERSON BEHIND THE PURPOSE

Grace! honor what an honor to meet you! You are a godly example of kindness and grace!! I pray this book is a blessing to you as you continue to walk in your great purpose!

Debra Byas
9/2022

DEBRA L. BYAS

"The Strong One": Godly Wisdom for the Person Behind the Purpose

Trilogy Christian Publishers
A Wholly Owned Subsidiary of Trinity Broadcasting Network
2442 Michelle Drive, Tustin, CA 92780

Manufactured in the United States of America
10 9 8 7 6 5 4 3 2 1
Library of Congress Cataloging-in-Publication Data is available.

ISBN: 978-1-68556-971-6
E-ISBN: 978-1-68556-972-3

DEDICATION

I give glory to God, my creator and the supplier of all that encompasses my life and world! His purpose is foremost in my life as I play my part in His divine design.

I dedicate this book to my husband, Carl E. Byas Sr. You are the wind on which I take flight and soar. You are the earthly example of God's love for me, my hero, and my closest friend. Father God sent you into my life when it seemed I was drowning because He knew you could reach me and would not let go even after I was above water.

Thank you for your love and support during my many projects and endeavors. All the late nights when you could have complained, but you saw the greater mission, ministry, and passion within me. When your time was full of home, career, and ministry responsibilities, you kept me as your primary responsibility in the earthly realm. I honor you, and I will always love you.

ACKNOWLEDGMENTS

To my children, Tamika, Carl, Whitney, Jerrod (son-in-law), Stephanie, and my grandson, Joshua: your support has been priceless. Each of you brings elements of support and love crucial to the foundation of my purpose here on the earth. I see each of you differently in my role as a mother. Each of you is unique and brings out the best in me. Thank you for your love, support, inspiration, and all you contribute to my purpose for being here and me.

To my mother and father, Dorothy T. Logan and Thomas R. Logan Sr.: although you are no longer with me on the earth, your impact will always be apparent and substantial. Without your instruction, influence, and love, I would not be walking within the fullness of God's wisdom in my life.

To my Ma Mary: thank you for availing yourself in your unique and selfless way and always being there when we need you. To my sister, Veronica, my brother, Thomas, and my sister-in-law, Kim: thank you all for always being who you are with me and for your consistent support, love, and encouragement.

To my close circle of spiritual sisters and spiritual daughters—you know who you are—I love every one of you very much. You each bring a source of encouragement and support from the Lord. I recognize and value what you provide. Let's keep pressing forward, for there is no time to look back: our purposes are always ahead!

To my coach, Rev. Paula Palmer Green: I don't have the words to express how much you have impacted my life. Thank you for the push I needed to get this book transcribed from my heart onto paper. God's intention for our connection is clear and substantial. This book is only one proof of your effect on my person and ministry.

Lastly, to my spiritual leaders, Bishop Dr. Joseph V. Garnett III and Lady Bregetta Garnett: thank you for your prayers, guidance, and selflessness in caring for the flock of God! You are examples of great leaders, and I admire you both for your strength and endurance. You are the *strong ones* in many lives!

CONTENTS

FOREWORD I

It is said that we are changed by the books we read, the places we go, and the people we meet. Pastor Debra is truly one who our Father has purposed to be a conduit for change in the lives of others, and it is my prayer that you will be changed by reading this book. It is an honor to know her and experience how God uses her to help others embrace their God-given purpose with efficacy and might. She embodies her namesake Deborah in the Bible, who was a judge, prophet, priest, and worshipper. As a prophet and judge, Deborah was said to hear God's voice and share His word with others. God used her to inspire His chosen people for a mighty victory over those who lived in the land He promised to them.

"The Strong One": Godly Wisdom for the Person Behind the Purpose provides practical, prophetic, yet applicable information not just for those who find themselves being the "one" who everyone comes to for answers and strength. It is a source of inspiration, motivation, and strategies rooted in the Word of God for those seeking to effectively live a life with purpose and victory.

In the marketplace, Pastor Debra is a skilled leader, builder, and strategist. She applies those same skills to ministry. Everyone around her experiences her compassionate mother's heart that extends beyond her family. It is because of who God made her to be and the call upon her life that she writes this book to help you continue to be strong and do the amazing things our Father made you to do. Every page is packed with wisdom to apply as you accept the challenge to push past how you perceive things, embrace what is written in God's Word, and know that you are made with, for, and on purpose.

This book will help you accept the challenge of being purposeful about expanding the kingdom of God within your span of influence.

Before anything happened on the earth, God spoke a word. The words on the following pages are God-given. Each declaration, prayer, prophetic letter, and self-reflective exercise contained within will inspire you to live life with more intentionality. You will be prompted to look within and look to our heavenly Father to find more meaning in your life. And in so doing, the plan our Father has for your life will become even more apparent.

God purposefully made you, and, according to His Word, He fashioned your days before they were formed (Psalm 139:16). Others are waiting for you to come forth in the fullness of who you were made to be. Reading this book will help you live bigger, shine brighter, and have a greater impact on the earth. As you turn the pages, you will find peace, power, purpose, and, most of all, honor in being the "strong one"!

—Rev. Paula Palmer Green
Founder and Overseer of Covet2Prophesy Ministries

FOREWORD 2

In 1993, as a marine, I was deployed on the USS *Saipan*. The one thing, apart from mealtimes, that was most looked forward to was hearing the mail call over the loudspeaker. We gathered like children on Christmas, hoping to have received a letter.

It never failed: those who received letters would steal away and sit with them. *"The Strong One": Godly Wisdom for the Person Behind the Purpose* nostalgically impacted me in the same way: as I began to read the letters, I found myself stolen away in a serene place for the purpose of sitting with my correspondence.

As you sit with the words of this book, they will broaden your capacity to accept the completeness of your purpose. More importantly, they will challenge your capacity to remain resilient. Be prepared for the necessary reminder—you are *the strong one!*

—Bishop Dr. Joseph V. Garnett III
Senior Pastor at Freedom's Way Ministries,
Wilmington, NC

INTRODUCTION:

"You Are The Strong One!"

How many times have you heard that? How many times did situations wait on you to handle them? You stepped in when others seemed not to have the courage, knowledge, resolve, or willingness to tackle the tough challenges that needed to be addressed. But you instinctively stepped up because it's what you do and it's who you are. It's as if you were made for these moments!

It mattered not that you never faced the type of challenges or circumstances that have found their way before you. You just knew you would find a way to resolve the crisis, often in a manner above the anticipation. Afterward, when you step back to consider how things unfolded, it always seems as if it was the expectation for you to be the fixer. It was an expectation not just from yourself but also from others around you. Why? Because *you* have always been seen as "strong."

Another statement you may often hear is, "I'm not as strong as you are." But why and how did you get this designation? Did God stamp the big *S* on your chest? What is it that you have that those others don't?

Most strong people secretly ask themselves, "Why do I seem willing to do what others do not?" It may appear that some just don't want to take the responsibility that you so readily accept. What is it that they see in you? What are you unwillingly or unknowingly showing them? What instinctive characteristics do you have that are struggles for others? You recognize a level of strength in you, but anyone who just exerts some effort can do the same thing! Right? And if everyone can do the same thing, why is it you to whom this distinctive title has been bestowed?

At the onset of this book, I want to emphasize that being a strong person does not necessarily mean having a strong personality. There are those with strong, or some may say, challenging or difficult personal characteristics. Those with strong personalities often put more emphasis on establishing how others should perform or act around them. But there is a difference between being strong inside and having a strong personality. Not all strong people have strong personalities, and some people with challenging personalities are not very strong inside. I would define strong people as those who instinctively step up when a situation needs to be handled in their area of strength. They know what to do or have the fortitude to forge through things others may not want or have the capacity to do.

You are "the strong one" and automatically a leader in your area(s) of influence. I know you accept that. However, frustration can come as others entitle themselves to your consistent willingness to step up. The expectations and entitlement may slow you down for a while, but you understand you must continue to step up because it is just what you do. It is part of how God has engineered you. It gives a definition and shape to the assignments within your purpose.

But at specific points of life, your heart cries out, "Who sees me? I'm tired of this expectation of supernatural strength, persistence, or resilience. Does anyone notice I'm hurting too?

How do I continue to carry and juggle things for others during my moments of intense internal struggle?"

You are strong because your creator established it as a big part of your purpose. You cannot stop being strong, just as you cannot stop the reason for which your creator purposed you. You cannot separate yourself from your purpose, for it is why you exist. It cannot be detached from you. It awakes when you awake. It stops when you stop. It dies when you die. Your legacies and establishments may continue, but your specific purpose is only here as long as you are. You must make sure you are sustained enough to carry out all that you have been endowed to complete. This ability goes beyond resilience, as there must be greater self-awareness and comprehension of how you operate within your strengths.

There were times when I knew burnout was inevitable if there were not a deeper level of understanding of how God wired me and expected me to manage and maintain myself within my greater purpose. These were issues and thoughts I had to address internally and honestly. I knew that if I wanted to continue to flow in God's purpose for my life, I could not shut off the stream of what I was to produce but, instead, continue to successfully produce while managing the person behind my purpose—myself!

This debut book is written to awaken you to the deeper intricacies of how you can be supported as the person behind your purpose. You are strong, but your strength will only take you to limited destinations. Your person must come before your role. You are a person before you are a leader, parent, spouse, counselor, or any other role you work within the purposes of God. If we try to build up the title roles without building up and sustaining the person, we will not hold up through the elements and pressures of life.

As I sat before the Lord, I asked for His supernatural endowment of prophetic encouragement for the readers of this book. As I placed my hands on the computer keyboard, the Holy Spirit spoke words directly to my spirit! Upon my return to read the words typed, it was as if I was reading them for the first time. I knew they were not from me. These prophetic words are presented as letters included before each chapter. I pray these words from God help reveal our Father's love for you as you walk in His divine blueprint for your life. I pray they speak to your spirit and soul.

Get ready to be challenged and to grow. Use the book's *positive declarations*, *wisdom nuggets*, and *prayers* to shift you into deeper levels of personal and spiritual insight. Prepare to discover details about yourself while developing a management plan focused on how you can be sustained as the strong person behind your powerful purpose!

PROPHETIC LETTER:

Why Do I Allow It

Beloved,

   I have called who you were before time. Before you were formed, I saw you as purpose... not just purposeful, but as My divine purpose.

   To walk effectively in who you are is not based on what you have experienced but on what you have accepted as part of each experience. I allow it for the experience. As difficult as that is, only your purpose can see more clearly than you can right now. Purpose stands up during your experiences and declares who you are. I allow it for the declaration of who you are.

   From the point of your conception, My purpose for you had a demand for you to stand in what I would allow. The pain, the loss, the grief, the despair, as well as the joy, the hope, and the love are just parts of the symphony of My purpose for you. Each experience expresses itself in a masterpiece that only I can create. So, don't faint in what I allow. Only I can hold you together—accept Me. Don't run from Me.

My Word declares the song I wrote about you. When you receive what I allow, you begin to hear it. The purpose in your life calls to Me.

Beloved, I have committed My work unto your hands, and I will not take My hand from yours. I allow it because people need your life's song. I am not the only one who hears it. Your song is for others, and their songs are for you.

You are complete in what I have allowed. Steal away and hear the song you are, and you will understand why I allow what happens in your life. You are a complex, masterful composition of My love. I conduct your song with perfect intonation. Each circumstance that was allowed came in and through My direction.

Listen to the whole song and not just one part, for then you will hear the completeness of My purpose for you. You will listen to My love, and you will listen to the song called "You."

Trust Me with each piece of your song. Even the dissonant parts have a beauty that fulfills and completes the melody with perfect intonation. I allowed it because I had seen you and heard your melody before you were born. It was good then, and it is good now.

Everything I do in your life is for a reason. So, even if you don't understand every part, just hear the completeness of your song. I'm speaking and will continue to talk with, and through, everything I allow in your life. Each experience has and will continue to work together to bring forth purpose, even if you don't understand it at the time.

Others can hear your song too. But I desire that you keep your ear ready to hear—not just the one instrument playing so loudly at this present time but the totality of your song—it's My love; it's My purpose for you.

CHAPTER I:

What Do Others See?

Then he said, "What have they seen in your house?"
So Hezekiah answered, "They have seen every-
thing that is in my house; there is nothing among my
treasuries that I have not let them see."
—Isaiah 39:4 (NASB)

This may be hard to swallow right out the gate, but here it goes. How well do you know yourself? Your first thought could be, *I know myself better than anyone else.* But...do you? It's hard to imagine that you may not fully know yourself until you unmask what others see in you. They see a leader, a trailblazer, and a closer; those are all factual statements about solid people. But underneath those assessments of your abilities, what else do others see inside your house? You may say, "I don't care what others see." But that could be a big mistake. Your effectiveness heavily depends on what others see in you, not solely on how you see yourself. You may have been told how strong you are but also struggle internally with that perception of yourself. Or maybe you know that you are strong but still wonder why you were chosen to be so. It seems to come to you naturally; therefore, it is difficult to understand why others don't just flow in the same strengths.

I have talked to many solid men and women in my journey, and one thing has stood out in common; understanding and acknowledging how others see them are tremendously under-valued and need attention. How others see us is crucial to our complete self-awareness and instrumental in determining our "purpose-awareness."

> Everything we do says something to someone.
> The things we don't do could say even more.

It's not just how we present ourselves outwardly, although that has a profound effect. Even when we are unaware, every-thing we show from within speaks to others about what we carry. What do others see in you?

We take great care, especially in this social-media age, to be confident in who we think we are and not to place too much emphasis on the opinions of others. Today, I read these statements on social media posts: "Stop worrying about what others think of you and just be yourself" and "Who cares what others think about you? It's only important what God thinks about you." Although both statements have elements of truth, neither is a good foundation of thought. As we already covered, what others think of you, whether good or bad, will reveal a great depth of understanding regarding your purpose here in the earthly realm. We are not here on the earth just for ourselves, a few friends who we know love us, and God! It goes beyond what we can box up within our mental capacities. Our purpose will be revealed in how we affect others, particularly those assigned to us. Even Jesus asked His disciples, "Whom do men say that I am?" (Mark 8:27, KJV).

Jesus was a very polarizing figure. He was either very loved or very hated. Notice He did not say, "Who do the *men that like and understand me* say I am?" He wanted the various statements regarding His effect within the earthly realm. It did not mean He didn't know who He was or was upset that some did not get who He was. Then Jesus asked His disciples, "*But* whom say ye that I am?" (Matthew 16:15, KJV). This was to hear the words of those in His circle as to what effect He had on those assigned to that season of His ministry. Both responses spoke to His purpose from God, regardless of whom each opinion came from.

In the context of the opening scripture to this chapter, Isaiah 39:4, Hezekiah was flattered at the interest and visit from the king of Babylon and his envoy. So much was Hezekiah flattered that his pride caused him to compromise himself and the safety of Judah as he boasted of his wealth to those who should have been seen as potential enemies. He arrogantly exhibited his power by showing potential enemies his wealth, massive food supplies, and significant and impressive military armaments. Hezekiah was later rebuked and admonished by the prophet Isaiah, who made him aware of the consequences that would follow his foolish act of pride. We may disapprovingly look at Hezekiah for letting his pride outweigh his intellect at that moment. I think it is safe to say most of us would not show everything to even our closest friends, as we understand the more that is seen, the more our vulnerabilities increase. Even more so, we would consider it foolish to show everything we have to potential enemies. But as I was thinking over this concept, it became apparent that we knowingly and unknowingly disclose what is inside us all the time! Just because we don't intentionally show a specific side of ourselves (let's refer to this as a room inside your house or you as a person), it doesn't mean people don't see what's in you. The people around us and those affected by us have seen everything in our house even when we don't think we have made it visible to them. We may not want to acknowledge that! We try so hard to keep our secrets and vulnerabilities in check. This scripture speaks to everyone, even if we don't want to admit it. "There is nothing among my [your] treasures that I [you] have not shown them [someone]."

> People *see* what is in your house,
> and *you* are the one that has shown them.

Some people have seen only one or two rooms, while others have been privy to almost every room. Therefore, while everyone does not know everything, collectively, everyone knows everything! All things have been uncovered. This can be an unsettling thought, but could this be God's ultimate plan that unveils His purpose so lovingly placed inside?

With that, let's go back to the question: Why are *you* "the strong one"? Exactly how did you happen to get that title? It's simple; you are strong in the areas/rooms where people *see* you as strong. Those are the areas that others see as a source of strength despite lacking self-awareness. It is these areas/strengths that people pull on the most. I call it *placing a demand on you and your purpose.* When people put a demand (even if it's an unspoken demand) on you, it's because they see a supply. One of the most popular and fundamental economic theories is that of "supply and demand." When people need something, they will seek a supply. The price (willingness to pay) increases when there is a demand or search for an item in short supply. When the supply exceeds the demand, the price/cost decreases. What are people willing to pay (not necessarily money) for what you provide? You should take inventory of the areas people see in you and, therefore, demand from you because they know what they need is in you—it's in your house. You cannot cover the light of God that He placed inside you!

> *No man, when he hath lighted a candle, covereth it with a vessel, or putteth it under a bed; but setteth it on a candlestick, that they which enter in may see the light. For nothing is secret, that shall not be made manifest; neither anything hid, that shall not be known and come abroad. Take heed therefore how ye hear: for whosoever hath, to him shall be given; and whosoever hath not, from him shall be taken even that which he seemeth to have.*
>
> —Luke 8:16–18 (KJV)

The Adversary Knows the Unbridled Power in Your Purpose

It is essential to understand what the adversary sees in you. The adversary loves for you to cover up the light of God within, as he is tremendously intimidated by you and your purpose. Why is this? Because he hates anything that God ordains. Satan knows your destined purpose will always fit within God's divine purpose for this world. As we know, Satan is always directly opposed to God's divine will and purposes. As the adversary knows the power in your purpose, so should you. In line with that, Satan opposes any path that provides revelation to you regarding your purpose! His strategy keeps you off-focus and confused about your purpose because your lack of knowledge in this area gives him a spiritual advantage. "My people are destroyed for lack of knowledge [...]" (Hosea 4:6, ESV). God's purpose is why you were born, and it is why you are still here. God saw a specific divine purpose in the spirit, then ordained you to fit that particular purpose in the natural realm. That means *your purpose* came first! As I teach all the time, the spiritual realm is the original realm, so things always start there first. The Bible is clear when it says, "And God said, 'Let there be'" (from the spiritual), "and there was" (in the physical). Nothing happens in the physical realm unless it first happens in the spiritual one. What we end up seeing and experiencing in the physical realm is always a manifestation of what has already happened in the spiritual world, whether divine or diabolical. The fullness of this revelation to humankind is dangerous to the strategies of Satan. He already understands that by the time we are fighting something by natural means, it has already happened in the spiritual dimension. He wants us ignorant of our God-ordained authority within our purpose to directly influence and affect what manifests in the earth. He does not want us to understand that we have the authority through prayer to shift spiritual occurrences according to God's divine plan before they physically manifest on the earth. This is why Jesus directed his disciples to pray forth God's will to manifest on the earth according to His divine will and purpose. Jesus directed them to pray on this wise: "Thy kingdom come. Thy will be done in earth, as it is in heaven" (Matthew 6:10, KJV).

You see, your purpose was already established as part of God's plan in the spiritual realm. But Satan's strategy is to keep us focused only on this natural realm, as he knows any spiritual plan has already been successful by the time we see it manifested on the earth. When we falsely think that Satan is fighting us simply because he doesn't like us or doesn't want us to have that new car/house/spouse we believe God for, it is inaccurate! Satan does not hate you simply because you have accepted Jesus Christ as your Savior and Lord. The adversary is not fighting against you. He is fighting against your purpose or, more directly, God's purpose! He doesn't just hate you because you are strong, but what he hates is the plan that you were born to fulfill. *You* are the *physical manifestation* of God's divine supernatural *purpose*. Satan is reminded of that each time he encounters you. He sees the physical manifestation of what he already fought against in the spiritual realm.

> Now it's time for us to know the power of the space for which we were born.

Satan knows how powerful our existence is, but when *we* see it, it muddles his strategy and, thereby, takes away certain advantages in the spiritual realm. When we are no longer focused on what has already physically manifested, and our focus shifts to strategizing on spiritual things, "If ye then be risen with Christ, seek those things which are above, where Christ sitteth on the right hand of God. Set your affection on things above, not on things on the earth" (Colossians 3:1:2, KJV), then we affect what manifests in the earthly realm. Rather than playing catch-up and praying for reversal, we set the tone of what physically manifests. We become part of the predestined victory that God has ordained in His purpose for us. We are victorious because God's purpose always ends in victory! We always win because God always wins. We prevail because God's Word always prevails! That's why Scripture tells us, "We know that all things work together for good [victory] to them that love God, to them who are the called according to *His purpose*" (Romans 8:28, KJV; emphasis and text in brackets mine). *It is all about your purpose!*

Identify What You Supply and How You Impact Others

Identifying what you supply to others enables you to determine what you have to offer and, even more so, what God has given you to contribute. Knowing how and what others see in you is key to how you capitalize on your strengths and go forward in God's purpose placed in you!

> *We are God's handiwork, created in Christ Jesus to do good works, which God prepared in advance for us to do.*
>
> —Ephesians 2:10, NIV

We are the handiwork of God. He has given everyone purpose, and He will not change His mind or remove His purpose from you. Very few people rightfully equate their "supply" to their "purpose." Purpose can never be selfish; however, many may unknowingly see it that way. They may see purpose as the way God created us to gratify ourselves. But God created you to meet the demands of those around you. We are all here to help meet needs and influence the lives of those exposed to us. Your purpose as a mother, father, sister, brother, friend, worker, mentor, counselor, leader, influencer, etc., has been given to you because someone demands it. What you supply to others is directly related to your God-given purpose. You were given your part to play in God's ultimate plan. How you package and lead others is directly related to the influential sphere in which God has placed you.

When my perception of my strengths came closer to what others saw in me, I not only saw what I supply but also uncovered my spheres of influence or spheres of impact. Your impact sphere is the environment where your strengths affect and give others permission to become more aware of why they are here! It is the area(s) that defines how you make your impression in this world. I quote it like this:

> Your purpose is the *part you play* in *His* purpose, and your *leverage* (influence) is *how you lead* others in *theirs!*

You have an advantage in your area of effect (leverage) that others don't. How well do you lead others to walk in their strengths and purpose? You will never know the extent of influence you have without knowing what you supply and how you impact others!

To See and to Say Are Different!

When determining what others see in us, we must understand that "see" and "say" are two separate words and concepts. They have distinct meanings regarding our reception of what others perceive about us that have long been erroneously accepted as synonymous. Let's no longer accept these words as equal. We must be able to receive what others see, but we also must be ready to interpret what others say! We often take offense by confusing this truth. How many of us have thought something but chosen to say a different thing that may be viewed as more acceptable or less uncomfortable for the hearer? In the same light, how many of us have said something that is deliberately opposite of what we see simply because we did not want to provide the affirmation or confirmation that the hearer was seeking? We must be able and ready to discern when statements need interpretation before we put ourselves in the position of receiving them. Not that we are to turn every word we don't like into one with a more pleasant meaning. We should be aware not to avoid hearing things we need to improve upon. But it becomes crucial to recognize when words don't align with our true nature or God-given personality. Pray for the discernment to process words that are said to you or about you.

There are times when you may misunderstand the words from others in their context. There are also times when others intentionally mishandle us through comments. Discernment and wisdom can avert the assignment of damaging words. Even unspoken language (i.e., body language, your entrance into a room atmosphere, etc.) can convey messages that must be discerned before they are received. Perceived messages from unspoken language are underestimated in their influence. The power people convey in what they do is significant and must be interpreted before the implicit messages are received.

Perspective Dilemmas Are
Common amongst Strong People

Our perspective is the lens through which we see things. It is our point of view regarding something. Many things shape and mold our perspectives; therefore, they are prone to change. When trying to determine or accept a God-given purpose, assignment, or even direction, we create a dilemma if we look through a flawed "self-perspective." Selfish or one-sided perspectives can keep you from efficiently walking in your purpose. You shouldn't depend on one or two friends or family members to shape the lens determining your point of view. What others *see* should not be brushed off or ignored. But be aware of receiving everything others *say* about you. Almost everything we think negatively about ourselves can likely be traced to what we have heard others say! The words spoken about us stick with us and affect us profoundly. Therefore, when we receive and accept bitter, twisted language into our ears, that can cause us to have a flawed perspective of ourselves, as we relate that language to what others *see* in us. It is because we falsely believe people always say what they see. As previously noted, to *see* and *say* are two different concepts. Missing or misinterpreting what others see can be the culprit creating a tainted perspective of who we are. When we receive things that do not reflect what God placed inside us, we can legitimately shut down from frustration and discouragement. When unkind, cruel words cause flawed perspectives, we must be able to shift the erroneous ones. There is a human perspective, and then there is God's perspective.

How do we make that shift? I see this move occurring in two phases. Firstly, we align our perspectives by accepting and receiving what God says to and about us. Secondly, we must know how to interpret and receive what humans say to and about us. This practice will help us see ourselves as God sees us and what God has gifted us to produce on the earth.

Accept God's Perspective

God has wonderfully and intentionally created us for a great purpose. He deeply desires us to know this. Throughout His Word, we find His desire for us to accept His perspective about His purpose for us.

> *And we have received God's Spirit (not the world's spirit), so we can know the wonderful things God has freely given us.*
>
> —1 Corinthians 2:12 (NLT)

God has given us purpose and inheritance for His glory and fulfilling His purpose. He has predestined us to fit perfectly into His purpose. According to the Word of God, His purpose came first; then, we were perfectly created to work within His established objectives for His glory.

It is glorious to see how God sees humanity. We are intricately designed within the more significant design of God. Accepting God's perspective requires giving time and attention to God and His Word! Time with God is never wasted time. The Bible outlines God's ultimate purpose and how our purpose is fitted within His. Have you ever asked God to show you who you are through His perspective? Not that we could attain everything God knows, but the Bible declares what He has freely given to us is ours to have.

As we comprehend, through the grace of God, our role in His plan and His desire to provide wisdom and revelation of our inheritance in His plan, it liberates us into accepting our purpose. With this in mind, how does God speak to you in the following scripture?

Blessed be the God and Father of our Lord Jesus Christ, who has blessed us in Christ with every spiritual blessing in the heavenly places even as he chose us in him before the foundation of the world, that we should be holy and blameless before him. In love, he predestined us for adoption to himself as sons through Jesus Christ, according to the purpose of his will, to the praise of his glorious grace, with which he has blessed us in the Beloved. In him we have redemption through his blood, the forgiveness of our trespasses, according to the riches of his grace, which he lavished upon us, in all wisdom and insight making known to us the mystery of his will, according to his purpose, which he set forth in Christ as a plan for the fullness of time, to unite all things in him, things in heaven and things on earth.

In him we have obtained an inheritance, having been predestined according to the purpose of him who works all things according to the counsel of his will, so that we who were the first to hope in Christ might be to the praise of his glory. In him you also, when you heard the word of truth, the gospel of your salvation, and believed in him, were sealed with the promised Holy Spirit, who is the guarantee of our inheritance

until we acquire possession of it, to the praise of his
glory.

For this reason, because I have heard of your faith
in the Lord Jesus and your love toward all the saints,
I do not cease to give thanks for you, remembering you
in my prayers, that the God of our Lord Jesus Christ,
the Father of glory, may give you the Spirit of wisdom
and of revelation in the knowledge of him, having the
eyes of your hearts enlightened, that you may know
what is the hope to which he has called you, what are
the riches of his glorious inheritance in the saints.

—Ephesians 1:3–18 (ESV)

Recognize Flawed Self-Perspectives

How we perceive who God is will ultimately color how we see His objective on the earth and determine our purpose for being here as His children. We need His perspective to be clear before understanding how we should see ourselves. Without this clarity, we can continue to walk in inaccurate self-perspectives. The word of God is evident in many passages of Scripture that our perspectives of the world, others, and ourselves can be imperfect.

God knew that we would have to deal with these inaccurate perspectives. I believe it is one of the many reasons why God made the Bible so readily available to us.

How can you say to your brother, "Brother, let me take
out the speck that is in your eye," when you do not see

the log in your eye? You hypocrite, first take the log out
of your own eye, and then you will see clearly to take
out the speck that is in your brother's eye.

—Luke 6:42 (ESV)

The eye is the lamp of your body; when your eye is
clear, your whole body also is full of light; but when it
is bad, your body also is full of darkness.

—Luke 11:34 (NASB)

Every way of a man is right in his own eyes: but the
LORD **pondereth the hearts.**

—Proverbs 21:2 (KJV)

God wants us to get the log out of our eyes to change our perspectives about others and ourselves. There will always be things and characteristics we see within ourselves that are not what God desires us to see. It takes the Word of God to expose these thoughts within our hearts and draw us into His truth of who we are in Him. Our recognition of the truth of God's Word over our current views, opinions, and judgments is an essential step in our purpose journey.

What Role Does Pain Have in Shaping Our Perspectives?

Knowing that we have a great and unique purpose from God is a critical initial step in discovering and operating in purpose. As we have been discussing, as we recognize the intricacies of God's intention within our purpose through the eyes of others, a dimension of revelation and enlightenment can follow. God knows how to surround us with those needing what we have to offer. Paul prays for the Ephesians "That [...] the eyes of your heart may be enlightened" (Ephesians 1:18, KJV). Others may see an extent of our strength(s) that we sometimes miss. We usually overlook characteristics that are strengths because, generally, there is great pain that has shaped and enhanced them. We naturally run away from pain, but the pain is a powerful force and developer of our strength. When I hear what others see as one of my strengths, I can always trace it back to moments of pain that catalyzed a reaction or momentum in me to overcome the pain. Take a moment to reflect on your most painful memories, and then ask yourself, "What did I do to the best of my ability to make sure this type of pain never happens to me or someone else again?" You can connect it with a developed strength if you trace it correctly.

My most painful childhood memories seemed to be associated with rejection. I was belittled due to my perceived body issues. I had darker skin than some others in my family. My darker skin was not an accepted quality of beauty, so I always saw myself as not being as attractive as others. I was taller than most of my acquaintances, so I felt oddly different and awkward. I was omitted and misunderstood even in what I considered my friend circle. I was extremely introverted, which did not lend well to socialization and added to feelings of rejection. I loved to hide in the background so that others did not notice me as an achiever even though I was academically gifted. In the household where I grew up, there were not a lot of affectionate displays, either privately or publicly. I had to learn how to hug. There was not much kissing or warm words like "I love you" in our family. I knew early in life that I had a love for learning. I studied a lot and found solace in books and education. One of my favorite places was school, and I excelled with little effort. Honor society, Governor's School, the top ten of my senior class, and other academic rewards and accomplishments gave me a sense of pride. Still, it was also the platform for another form of rejection from peers who did not perform as well and were, quite frankly, envious of that ability in me.

The introverted, not feeling pretty, awkward, misunderstood, and unable to outwardly display affection carried on throughout my teenage life and into college. My prayer became for God to endow me with the acceptance and confidence I needed to ensure I had a purpose. For inner acceptance, I found myself needing to exceed expectations in everything I did. Everything I did had to be top-notch and excellent. It had to be great and above all else. It was better to be rejected because of jealousy than not being good enough. So, I made sure everything was in that spirit of excellence. I needed to be confirmed because I did not get confirmation from my family and peers. They rarely told me who I was or confirmed who I thought I was. So now, I recognize some of my most considerable areas of strength were produced from my most significant moments of pain. I realized I carried myself well because I had to overcome my low self-image. I understand the love people feel when I hug them because I can relate to the pain caused by not experiencing the love of a healing hug when I was younger. I realized my draw toward those that felt broken and rejected was because I was once broken, rejected, and abandoned. I see the potential in others because I know how it felt not to be seen for what I carried inside.

Others see me as a mentor and a confirming presence in their lives. They tell me that I carry myself with a certain grace and confidence that inspires them to follow the example I display. They tell me that I can see potential in them that they could not see. They tell me I accept them for who they are and appreciate my focus is to push and inspire them to go farther than what is considered average. They tell me that I am a consistent supply of wisdom and knowledge presented with a spirit of excellence. Once I comprehended that what others saw in me was evidence of God-given purpose (what I supplied to them), I was motivated to confidently operate as a pastor, mentor, spiritual mother, leader, and other roles within my purpose. I operated well in each role because of the pain I experienced. God allowed the past painful experiences so that I could be successful in my current assignments.

How Do You Assess What Others See in You?

I'm not an advocate of encouraging people to solicit statements from others regarding what they see or think of them. When we do that, the responses we receive are scripted at best and incomplete at worst. Instead, I want to help shift a common mindset that some people have. You may have heard it said not to take in words or statements from those that don't accept or work directly against your purpose. But instead, *only* listen to those trusted individuals who love and glean from you. However, we need to hear from both elements of people because your enemies see the same things that your friends and supporters see. Enemies may sabotage and try to scar the image of what they see in you. But they still see the same things in you that speak to your purpose because they see what's in your house.

I stated you don't need to stop at this point and ask people what they see and think of you because it has already been told! As in the opening scripture, Hezekiah confessed regarding his potential enemies "They have seen all that is in my house; there is nothing among my treasuries that I have not shown them" (Isaiah 39:4, ESV). Just know that people *see* what is in you even if they don't come out directly and confirm the positive things they see. Statements or actions from those who don't like you reveal what they *see*: for you have shown it to them, and they see it! Your strengths will uncover friends, enemies, as well as frenemies. Here is what we sometimes don't understand: we need *all* of them! Your "enemies" see the same things your friends see. They may sabotage or twist your strengths to minimize or undermine you or your purpose.

> The comfortable thing to do is ignore what we hear from enemies. But instead, we must learn to stop *ignoring* what people say and start *interpreting* what they say.

For example, if a friend sees that you are knowledgeable, with sound wisdom and judgment, you may often hear things like, "Thank you for listening to me. I love getting your advice because you see things at a level I did not think about, and it helps me greatly!" However, from an enemy, you may hear, "you don't know everything even if you think you do! Another great quote people may use against you when they see a knowledge gift in you is, "People don't care how much you know until they know how much you care" (Theodore Roosevelt). Even though there is truth in this, it does not cover every situation. I don't have to know how much an anesthesiologist cares about me as a person. Most of them have only met you for the first time on your surgery date. I only want them to know what the heck they are doing! I need their knowledge more than how much they care about me as a person. The positive and negative statements can be interpreted and reveal the same quality in you. There is a high level of knowledge and wisdom in your "house." So, understand that you must not ignore every uncomfortable statement; some just need to be interpreted.

I encourage you to take a journey into what you have already experienced and heard from others. Think intently and honestly about what others say around you and about you. Can you identify some phrases others say to you routinely or somewhat often? Here are some examples:

POSITIVE STATEMENTS OR QUESTIONS	STATEMENTS OR QUESTIONS NEEDING INTERPRETATION	POSSIBLE CHARACTER QUALITIES SEEN	POSSIBLE BIBLICAL GRACE/ GIFTING SEEN
May I have your advice about what I should do about this? If this were you, what would you do?	You don't know everything! You are not the only one that knows what should be done.	Respectful Influential Responsible Wisdom Good judgment Resourceful	Teacher Pastor Leadership
I feel comfortable talking with you; I can tell you anything. When I speak with you, it's as if I've known you forever.	You are too nice to people, and they will take advantage of you. You need to stand up for yourself more.	Relatability Trustworthy Warm Loving Positive	Pastor Counsel Leadership Encouragement
I don't know if I could have done what you did. Weren't you scared? I would have never been able to do that!	You are doing so much… why can't you focus on one thing at a time? Who do you think you are?!	Daring Faith Courage Assertive Ambitious Focused	Apostle Gift of faith Leadership Working of miracles

POSITIVE STATEMENTS OR QUESTIONS	STATEMENTS OR QUESTIONS NEEDING INTERPRETATION	POSSIBLE CHARACTER QUALITIES SEEN	POSSIBLE BIBLICAL GRACE/ GIFTING SEEN
Thank you for being so consistent and caring in your approach and advice to me. Thank you for always taking your time with me. I feel so special and loved around you.	You can't rescue everyone! You need to think of yourself sometimes!	Perceptive Great listener Compassionate Honesty Encourager	Teacher Word of wisdom Gifts of healing Gifts of help Ministry Service
Would you pray with/for me? I know God hears you! How did you know I was dealing with that issue?	Get up off your knees and do something about things. You are not the only one close to God. I hear God too.	Respect Faithfulness to God Trust Profound honor for the things of God	Gift of faith Prophet Word of knowledge Prayer or Intercession Ministry Service Worshiper

Accept the Authentic You

Accept the real you and guard against conforming to images other than your authentic self! Especially considering the overwhelming climate caused by social media. It is easy to fit yourself into someone else's character or area of influence, which may not necessarily be authentic to who you are. If you are not a people person, don't compare yourself to an extroverted salesperson just because they tell you how easy it is to do what they do. You will most likely not get the same results! It is outside of who you are. Be consistently aware of remaining *authentic* ("of undisputed origin; genuine"[1]) to who you are and not to whom you admire. You were not called to *conform* ("to act in accordance with expectations; to behave in the manner of others, especially as a result of social pressure"[2]). Instead, you were created to transform the lives of others.

If you find yourself conforming to the characteristics of whom you admire or even to the expectations of others for which you must manufacture a supply, you end up unauthentic. However, when you accept who you are in your strengths, it is *confirming* ("to give new assurance of the validity of: remove doubt about by authoritative act or indisputable fact"[3]) to you that you are fully walking in your God-given purpose.

Be courageously authentic in your person and purpose so you can experience the peace and freedom to walk in the highest degree of all that God has endowed you with. Doing so will likewise permit others to do the same.

Prayer

Father, I thank You for creating me for Your purpose. I know that You have intentionally made me who I am, and I accept Your plan for my life. Help me discover all You have placed within my sphere of influence. Give me a listening ear to hear how others see the purpose You put in me. Help me understand any pain You allowed was to establish the purpose You already placed in me. I need Your grace to produce what You have given me to supply to others. Help me do that with love and moral excellence. In Jesus's name, I pray. Amen.

Wisdom Nugget

Each day brings the opportunity to realize purpose and advance in it. Live each day knowing this and intentionally look for fulfilling your purpose today and each day. Do not cower from how others see you or define you when it aligns with what God has spoken over you. Recognize and operate purposely in your sphere(s) of influence.

My Declaration

My purpose is the part I play in God's purpose. I intentionally live out my purpose today, knowing I supply something to others in the unique way I was designed to operate.

PROPHETIC LETTER:
The Hidden Tears

Beloved

I see you—not just the parts you show others but the deepest crevice/cave you have constructed. It is a place where tears are not forced. It is a place that sometimes you refuse to see. But I am Jehovah Roi who sees even in the deepest of your hidden places. Of course, I see your open tears. But I also see the hidden ones. I have placed each of your tears in My bottle and put them in My book. They speak for the parts of you that only tears know how to express. The feelings you talk about and those you don't talk about or admit. The fears that clog access to your vulnerabilities. I see the tears that never make it to your tear ducts. Even when they don't fall from your face, they are there in the spirit. I am the God who conquers even through your weaknesses. There is not always a demand for physical tears. They are the unseen tears that never form but tears that still speak to me. You must know that I have given you all of them as a release, even as a sacred release to Me. I am your God, and I number each one. I am your comfort and strength when there are open tears. They express to me what you feel. But I am your heavenly Father who will not demand an explanation when you don't feel anything.

You ask, "Where are my tears?" I already know their location. I always see their message. I keep all of them. As you heed and complete My assignments, lean on My strength. You will then show My strength, which never questions the open or hidden tears because I gave you both.

CHAPTER 2:

Where Are My Tears?

One day I asked myself, "Where did my tears go?" I can't or don't seem to cry when an emotional situation would typically call for tears in many other people. Was I just trying to "never let them see me cry"? No. It almost seemed as if there was no instinct in me to cry. It was unusual and uncomfortable for me when I could not find the tears. I pondered this about myself to great lengths.

I know I was not born that way. I was always the crybaby in my family. I received an award for being the class crybaby in the third grade. It was the first of many graduation ceremonies that I can remember. Seeing all the award certificates passed out to my classmates. I sat wondering, *Will I get one too?* I waited with eager anticipation. Suddenly, the teacher announced the next award: "This next award goes to the biggest class crybaby of the year." Everyone laughed right at the onset of that announcement, including me. I wondered to myself, *Who is going to get that one?* But when *my* name was called, I couldn't figure out if I was happy that at least I was getting a reward or sad because of the embarrassment that came with it! I walked up to the front of the room to receive my prize. As I turned around, I saw the faces of the people watching me with sheer amusement. Suddenly, the flood of tears just came.

I could not hold them back. Everyone, including my mother, got a picture at that moment! That picture is still ingrained in my memory—it was as if it was a setup. My tears were proof of why I was receiving this ignominious honor.

I can laugh about it now, and the truth is, I have always been a hypersensitive person. I still am. But after some extremely tough life experiences, I realized I desired to solve problems rather than cry regarding them. I equated the tears with accepting a situation I did not want. Rather than cry, I put that energy into solving the problems as they came to me. *Now*, here I was, wondering where my tears were! There were times when tears were *needed* from *me*. There was a release that I was not giving myself through my tears. But after years of being the strong one, I was tearless. I was not emotionless but tearless nonetheless.

Why can't I cry? When you get accustomed to challenging situations, you condition yourself to hold yourself together so that things can get handled. If everyone falls apart, there would be no one to provide guidance, comfort, direction, or stability in a messy situation. Someone has to hold it together. It's almost like being the designated driver at a bar. The one that cannot drink or indulge so that others can return to their destination safely.

> Strong people are the designated drivers when critical problems arise. They are not staggering or emotionally compromised when sensible awareness is required.

They are the ones that people look to for the right words and the accompanying right actions. After this kind of conditioning, it was not surprising that I couldn't seem to find tears. You may be aware of this regarding yourself. You are not a rigid, unemotional person. You are just conditioned to fix things first.

One of the few places where I can be the crybaby that still resides in me is when I'm in the presence of the Lord. There, the tears come easily and often. I do not try to stop them. I don't have to be the voice of reason. I don't have to be the fixer. I don't have to be the designated driver. This is my place of release. Once, approximately fifteen years ago, I visited a church and encountered a minister who saw me weeping while at the altar during prayer. After the prayer was ended, the minister proceeded to tell me the expectation was to be happy in the presence of the Lord because the Bible stated that in His presence was the fullness of *joy*. He then said, but you seemed so sad! Why are you unhappy in the presence of the Lord? I thought about what he said, and at first, I thought maybe my tears were tears of joy! Well, that wasn't the case. So, I evaluated my tears. What was going on with me? Was I sad? No, I was, however, *full!* It was like a flood that was backed up as I expressed myself in the presence of my Father! After a few days, I realized God's love and presence created a place of release for me. When I'm in the presence of His *love* (for God is love), that becomes my place of freedom! Just because the Word declares that in His presence is the fullness of joy doesn't mean that other emotions cannot be expressed there. His presence carries the fullness of emotional release, peace, love, patience, gentleness, affirmation, and anything else we can pour out and receive from God.

May the presence of God be your most intimate place of release! It's about emotional balance. It's not a female thing to cry. I'm also speaking to the males considered strong in their spheres of influence. You must find places of *release!* If it is not in church, it's okay! Be you male or female—find the place where you can release the tears, whether they are open or hidden tears. Each type of tear expresses emotions. God sees them all.

What Were You Taught from Your Tears?

Pain will teach you lessons that last a lifetime. These "pain lessons" can affect the way we release our emotions. The spectrum of emotional displays is vast and, to a large degree, based on each person's life experiences. Some people identify emotional displays as a sign of weakness. For others, the need for extraordinary empathy, especially during difficult times, is essential. A vast spectrum of characteristics can emerge due to the lessons taught by pain. Character attributes range from being dangerously recluse to having excessive attention-seeking behavior. These behaviors are in part formed from the classes taught by pain. But one of the most incredible things we need to know is that we should keep expanding and maturing, especially in how we perceive ourselves.

Often strong people need to unlearn some of the self-protecting attributes that were created and learn how to be more vulnerable in their emotional expressions.

The bottom line is that vulnerability is expressed when we cry. You may be like me in that you are uncomfortable showing the fragility and vulnerability of emotional release except in very few people's presences. Past experiences have taught us tears don't solve anything. Others may believe the adage that strong people should never let others see them cry. Regardless of why tears may not come easy, you must find a place and space to release tears.

Why Do You Need to Release the Tears?

Tears are necessary and beneficial. You must know *why* it is needed to release them, *when* you need to release them, *how* to release them, and *to whom* you should release them. There must be a space where you can be vulnerable enough to cry. We all may know there are lots of physical benefits to crying. Releasing tears help to release tension and stress; it improves our mood and biochemical balance and brings an overall physiological balance. I believe it is crucial to be able to cry. Don't keep handling or finding a way to cope with intense emotions. If we don't know how and when to release, our bodies will eventually succumb at times that are not what we consider optimal. I know that I can release in prayer. Maybe you can let them go while watching a movie. Perhaps it is while reading or watching a sunset. It may be in the beauty of mountain top scenery or the peace of your backyard—the Lord is in all places. Music helps create a powerful backdrop for releasing all kinds of emotions. Whenever and wherever you find the suitable space(s) for you, then do it and do it routinely. The how of release varies from person to person and, at different times, within the same person. There is a broad spectrum that ranges from soft sniffles to uncontrolled wails. Whichever part of that spectrum calls for your tears, give yourself consent to yield to it. Whether public or private, release them.

Public versus Private Release

Some can release sensitive things openly and publicly (i.e., on social media). If this is true for you, be aware you must accept responsibility for how those who follow you perceive your vulnerability or openness, which involves taking the positive and negative responses once you release them. Others are very private and need a trusted personal circle of people who can support them in the way they need. If I choose to release open tears outside of the presence of God, I am thankful that He surrounds me with those who can handle and support me in them. They are rare and precious. I am unable to release them in the presence of just anyone. And I'm learning to be okay with the times that I can release emotionally.

Prayer

Father God, thank You for knowing me so well that You see the tears I cannot cry and not just the ones I can. And I also thank You for providing me the place(s) in which I can release the tears that fall within and from my eyes. I know the open and the hidden tears have meaning and represent a place in my heart that I am offering You. Help me release everything to You. You are my creator, so You know me intimately. Help me in the places that I hold in and become hardened. Send me the right people who understand and support me. Help me release my soul to cry! In Jesus's name, I pray. Amen.

Wisdom Nugget

Acknowledge where you stand in your ability to release yourself and your emotions. Find the space, opportunities, and support needed for you to be emotionally balanced. Do not limit or criticize yourself when the open tears don't come; you now know God sees all the inner cries of your heart.

My Declaration

I give myself space and permission to feel and release my tears and the emotions of my heart.

PROPHETIC LETTER:

Designed Capacity

Beloved,

As an instrument and carrier of My glory, I created you as a vessel. As the potter, I am the one that established and ordained your capacity. It was not your decision but Mine as your creator. As My vessel, you are limited in that you are not bottomless. The fact that you cannot carry everything that comes before you is not an indication of an inability to carry; it is just a reminder of the limits I have established. Don't compare your capacity to others, for I have given each vessel its dimensional imprint. When you compare, you overfill and take on too much. Lighten your load; I provide you with permission to respect your capacity. Take comfort that I have determined your limitations. I have defined that for you so that you wouldn't have to do so. It would be too much or too little if you had to determine how much to carry. Therefore, I say, I have done that for you. Trust the capacity I have established and ordained for you. Trust Me when you feel you can take a little more, but I pull you out because I know you should not try to carry it. Trust Me when I ask you to back up and say no. Saying no is not a statement of inability; it is an extension of My protection and Me. I am your shield as well as your refuge. Don't hesitate to come to Me for strength, guidance, and perseverance.

I look throughout the earth and ask, why are you doing that to yourself? Although I have given you creativity, I did not ordain the pressure you have placed on yourself to beat and conquer everyone around you. I did not direct the path that caused you to challenge My intentions when I designed you. You were wonderfully created in My image and likeness but not in My capacity. I made you with limits. I called you out of the expanse of the atmosphere as a creature that would contribute a designed purpose at a designed place and time. You are beautifully made. When did it become not enough for you? When did it spark the competition and comparison that you feel? It is My order and design to complete My intentions and purposes through you. When did My intentions become not high enough, not grand enough? I called out to you. I called to the you who I created. But you did not answer. The person you created in moments of competition and comparison emerged. You were determined and defiant to be...to be what you thought was acceptable. Acceptable to whom? You are already acceptable to Me. I created you in My image. I confirmed and affirmed you before you were formed. Look to Me to affirm you, for I am your creator. Breathe in My presence. Incline your ear to hear My whispers of who you are. You will hear My whispers as you shield yourself from the noise of comparison and competition. Please don't ignore them—it is Me.

CHAPTER 3:

The Machine Complex—You Are Not a Machine!

A s a strong woman who has had to prove herself in a highly competitive world, I have instinctively placed high expectations upon myself. I am enormously aware of this characteristic. I am conscious that this has not always been a beneficial thing and indeed not a healthy thing to do. This was a challenging chapter for me, as it required me to expose this about myself. Once while I was in complete meltdown mode due to almost unrealistic expectations from superiors at my job and my extreme need to prove that I could not only keep up but also exceed any expectation, my husband stepped in as a voice of reason. After listening to my determination to prove myself in this hostile climate, he said five words that have stuck with me since that day. He held my hand, looked me in the eye, and said, "You are not a machine." What a defining moment for me! Of course, I wasn't a machine. But my unrealistic expectations placed me in a superhuman position, and it took those words for me to realize what I was doing.

Since that day, I have had to recognize when I'm operating out the "machine complex." What do I mean? The Merriam-Webster dictionary defines the word "complex" as:

- a group of repressed desires and memories that exerts a dominating influence upon the personality
- an exaggerated reaction to or preoccupation with a subject or situation[4]

In other words, it's a strange and conflicting way of seeing yourself as something that you are not or something that you are not meant to be, thereby causing extreme and unconventional thinking and behavior. I wanted to be a superwoman. But superwoman is a fictional comic book character with superhuman abilities that are not vulnerable to human limitations. Much like a machine, I was in constant superhuman mode. And like a machine, I was over my capacity and breaking fast. *But* this never removed the feeling of knowing that I could do it. If others can, then why can't I? Why can't I be the first if no one has ever accomplished it? Why can't you do it all? With what or with whom was I trying to compare or compete? When you are seen as strong and understand that expectation of you, not only do people think you can handle everything, but you also tend to believe the same. This is undoubtedly an ambitious quality that others may see as a great thing, but there is a danger in this thinking when our human capacity is not considered. Capacity is the maximum quantity that something or someone can contain or carry. Capacity is also a quality that changes as our physical, emotional, and psychological climates change. For example, we may have a larger capacity to work and exert physical energy if our bodies are well and strong.

However, an episode of the flu can diminish our physical capacity the next week, and we find that the simple tasks we did not struggle with the week prior now exceed our present capacity. Therefore, we must be aware of and manage ourselves during fluctuations in our emotional, mental, and physical capacities at any given time. There will always be consequences to trying to exceed capacity.

> We should not look at capacity in the same light as a limitation. Limitations can be surpassed, but capacity certainly cannot!

The Capacity of Our Outward Man Reflects the Strength of Our Inner Man

The Lord speaks to us about the condition of our spirit or inner man. His Word lets us know His strength is made perfect in our weakness. Another way of saying that is His fullness is only realized when we realize our limited capacity! We have exhausted ourselves and exceeded our capacity because we have been accustomed to doing everything in our strength. But we need to ask God to teach us how to recognize the extent of what we can hold! As this book is being written, we are at the end of the COVID-19 pandemic that began over two years ago in 2019. We are coming out of a global shutdown and shut-off time! It has been a time of extreme change and heavy spiritual activity. I told God, "Surely You knew this was coming." And of course, He did! This is not an unexpected occurrence to God.

But even in this time when the world has quieted itself, we have found ways to fill things back up! I can almost say that I was busier in the worst stages of the pandemic because I learned how to fill my days with the noise of busyness and distractions. I filled myself with voices, entertainment, work, hobbies, and even ministry! God started to deal with me because I was reaching out to Him for answers about what was going on with me. He was still inside, but the overflow of Him was not there. I had less human capacity because I was so busy with fillers. He let me understand that He would not compete for my time and availability; I had to empty the outer things and create time for God to fill my inner man. I needed to recognize my need for physical and emotional rest.

How to Identify the Machine Complex

Strong people usually carry the weight of numerous things and several people most of the time. What is not realized or acknowledged is that we were never created to hold the amount of weight that we sometimes try to carry. It's not until we experience issues or consequences of the excess weight that we start to realize how much it affects us. Sometimes, despite the red flags we experience, we still don't understand that the extra weight is too heavy. We start to experience the red flags of breakdown. The emotional outbursts and collapses, and the "can everybody just leave me alone" moments! Physical red flags can also emerge. Effects of stress and constant exertion will manifest in physical symptoms and illnesses. These may be red flags that what we are attempting to carry is too much.

Flags that the capacity by which our creator gave us is being constantly pushed or challenged.

> If we are honest, strong people create coping mechanisms to deal with the excessive load we think we are supposed to hold.

When we have outbursts, meltdowns, uncharacteristic thoughts, illness, anxiety, etc., we create ways to shift, repackage, or subjugate the weight. Almost as if we don't have time to pay attention to the warning flags. So, the weight continues to build. The pressure keeps mounting, and we keep coping. Even if the coping consists of just ignoring our position of overload or turning to dangerous habits like drugs, sex, and alcohol. The outbursts and coping mechanisms show that something is excessive and needs to be released or eliminated. We have to realize that some things have to be eliminated, and we should no longer find a way to cope with it. Just a note that extra and undue weight may be in the form of people, places, or things.

> *Come to me, all you who are weary and burdened,*
> *and I will give you rest. Take my yoke upon you and*
> *learn from me, for I am gentle and humble in heart,*
> *and you will find rest for your souls. For my yoke is*
> *easy, and my burden is light.*
> —Matthew 11:28–30 (NIV)

I'm not saying we should only take care of ourselves. There will always be some weight outside ourselves—the responsibilities of children, family, aging parents, etc. Sometimes we may need to carry those unable to handle their weight: those with heavy addictions, disabilities, and incapacities outside their control. These are long-lasting and weighty loads that solid people have to carry due to the inabilities of those we love. But then some people are not pulling their weight because it's been handed to you or you have decided to take it. Now you've got their weight, your weight, and every other weight you feel God has created you to juggle. We feel the external and internal expectations. They come from those that pour out onto you externally and pull from you internally. There is an expectation in yourself and others that you always find a way to carry heavy loads, all while not breaking. These extreme loads are not the expectation from God. It should be nothing less than bizarre that we feel this is God's will for us to hold everything we pull in. We should ask for release from this kind of thinking.

How Did I Create and Fortify Expectations from Others?

You will find that people tend to keep loading things upon you as a strong person. Because you carry so well, your issues are either ignored or minimized. Even when there should be support, concern, or defense for you in a public arena, people will forgo and choose to defend someone they think appears weaker since they believe you can handle it independently without their display of support. They may come to your side privately, but the public nondefense can hurt. If you have encountered that situation, you find yourself asking why people come to you privately when the public support at the moment of the incident was needed. It is unfair, and it is a misuse of the emotions of a strong person. It can hurt even through strength. People assume this type of action will be continuously dismissed. The expectation is that you will keep looking past or overlook those actions. It is an expectation that a solid outward image has helped create in many ways. As strong men and women, we find it is essential to be able to take responsibility for some of the expectations that we have helped to create, both external and internal. Although unknowingly executed by us in most situations, the first step in dealing with overwhelming and unrealistic expectations is to start removing our participation in their creation, evolution, and perpetuation.

A Created Sense of Entitlement

A major internal frustration a strong person may have is when there is an expectation of caring for everybody else regardless of the personal cost. The cost is not always money. It can be time, energy, or other types of resources that are overbearing or overreaching. The expectation to carry others at your expense is common and seen as what you should do. There is an implied entitlement. Even when other people are around, the assumption is that you are the one that is okay and well able to provide the required result with no question. In all appearances, you seem to be handling things very well. Even when you are not okay, you find a way to care for your needs or at least the majority of them yourself. When people see that, even if they know you are not okay, they expect you to be whole enough provide them with what you produce and instinctively take care of yourself simultaneously. This is a dangerous image for you to portray, even if you are unaware. It is partly what you have established and will only be demolished once you stop fortifying it. Don't wait until you have a meltdown, blowout, or illness before you recognize your capacity has been exceeded: "Does anybody see *me*? Is there anybody here to take care of *me*?"

I love God because He is aware of our needs. He knows that we need other people in our lives. God is our source, but He also resources out human help. It is up to us to take up the help that He sends. There are some people we need to permit to help us recognize our capacity, and others need to be removed as recipients from the production line. We subconsciously think it is okay for others not to step in and help when we feel overloaded or overwhelmed. There is a need to shift some from the entitlement perspective and give permission to others to help you. Sometimes it may be a need to confront; other times, it may happen through friendly conversation. Whatever works for the situation, permit those who can help take care of some of your load and adjust the depiction of yourself that would allow people to expect something beyond your willingness or capacity to provide at any given time.

What Are Our Excuses for Why We Keep Exceeding Self-Capacity?

In coming to terms with recognizing the limitations that are part of our humanity, we will need to be able to hear and manage all of the excuses as to why "just this time" we need to push ourselves beyond our capacity. Remember: our capacity can ebb and flow depending on the physical, emotional, and psychological climates that we are in at any given time. When we understand the changing dimensions of our capacity, it allows us to come to terms with that human side of us without the impression that we are being heartless when we make others aware that we will not participate, contribute, be in charge, or otherwise extend the same service *at this time*. It is all a part of permitting yourself to say no to yourself before you can say the same to others. This is a way to know that you are healing from the process of continuously breaching your current capacity.

Prayer

My Father and my God, I thank You for making me with the capacity I needed for Your purposes to be completed in me. Help me when I feel the need to push myself beyond what I can accomplish well. I trust Your voice when you speak to my spirit to pull back. Forgive me and help me whenever I feel the urge to compete with the capacities of others. In Jesus's name, I pray. Amen.

Wisdom Nugget

Recognize when the expectations of yourself are outside of your current capacity. When you feel overwhelmed, it may indicate that you have exceeded a limit. Commit to being honest with yourself, taking the time you need for appropriate rest and restoration.

My Declaration

My total capacity has already been determined by Father God. I recognize and operate effectively within my current capacity today.

PROPHETIC LETTER:
This Far and No Farther!

Beloved,

As I have established you, I have established your call. There are areas within your call and regions outside of it. You and your call are just as I have purposed them. As I watch over My Word to perform it, you must watch over what I have created in you. You must guard it, manage it, and tend to it. Not just pray over it but protect it. I have set borders on the earth and in the spirit. When I set boundaries on the earth for the sea, I commanded that it could only come to its designated border and no farther. When I set borders in the spirit, I limit the authority and the access devils can attain.

I have permitted you to walk in My delegated authority in the same manner. Permission granted to walk in power to set borders within and boundaries over what I have given you. Just as I put the limits on the sea, I have granted you the authority that speaks to an adversary and says, 'This far may you come and no farther!' You have the authority to command who must stop and who can come closer. Use the power I have given you to command what comes and goes from you. You have permission to command what has access to you. You have permission to restrict or release what tries to access your atmosphere. Use the authority I have granted to fulfill the purposes I gave to you. Guard your calling and contents as much as you guard your physical possessions. Again, I say: permission is granted.

"The Strong One": Godly Wisdom for the Person Behind the Purpose

CHAPTER 4:

Produce and Protect

Our desire is not that others might be relieved while you are hard pressed, but that there might be equality. At the present time your plenty will supply what they need so that in turn, their plenty will supply what you need. The goal is equality, as it is written: "The one who gathered much did not have too much, and the one who gathered little did not have too little."
—2 Corinthians 8:13–15 (NIV)

Manage Output and Guard Access

In this chapter, I want to provide a framework regarding two major concepts regarding our God-given purpose: output and accessibility. Our output is what we produce, supply, or deliver to others. Everyone can be a supply to someone else's needs. But when you are considered the strong one in any area, there is increased demand, which inherently calls for increased output or production. Therefore, what you produce can quickly go into overdrive before you realize it. How many people depend on your ability to create what they need? Our *accessibility* (capability of being reached, quickly approached, or obtained) determines how easily others can gain admittance to you and what you supply.

Strong people may have difficulty limiting their output and accessibility, as both inherently increase as the demand for them increases. So, let's discuss output and accessibility. Both words are distinctly different but directly interconnected because as one increases, so can the other. There is an undeniable cyclic effect. The more you increase the supply of a demanded item (your output), there is an attraction to more people in need of your production, which opens the door to more people wanting access to you. As accessibility increases, so does the demand for your output. When you are strong in any specific area, your supply comes quickly and often. It comes more easily to you than others that do not possess the same strength and capacity. Your output attracts more people to demand access to you, which may become very weighty. The amount of weight you carry can be unnoticeable by you at; first, that is until the infamous "straw" breaks "the camel's back." For example, if you are a great listener, people will want to talk to you. The art of empathetic listening comes easily and effortlessly for you. People are attracted to your ability to hear beyond what others can listen and relate to. But listening takes time and energy that others may not recognize. People unload and release while you provide what they need—a listening ear and an empathetic response. When you make yourself and your time available, you give people access to you and your time. As more people discover your ability (usually through word of mouth), there is increased demand for your output. It comes so easily for you; it only becomes noticeable when the lack of time in other areas of your life becomes affected.

When operating within our purpose, managing production and protecting accessibility are essential to physical and mental wholeness. There must be intentional management and organization of our output and our accessibility.

> If you have not already, you should start with giving yourself the right to examine the importance of what you provide to others and how you allow others access to you and what you provide.

The use of the small and powerful word "no" is essential for everyone and is no different for a strong person.

You may be saying that you don't have an issue telling people no. I hear this phrase from a lot of strong men and women. The problem may not be with telling others no; instead, the "no" we fail to say to ourselves is what gets us in the overwhelming situation where expectations outweigh our output ability. It is intuitive and second nature for people to supply others with what they are good at producing. This is simply because of the ease with which we can operate in our strengths. I hear statements like "I have my boundaries that no one crosses" or "I've learned that I can't let people keep using me, and I know when to put my foot down and just say no," but do you? If you read chapter one and did an entire inventory on those areas of strength that you supply, you will find that because that strength comes more effortless for you, it is easy to turn on that strength without completely understanding how to "turn it off." People pleasers are not the only ones that find it hard to say no. I believe most "strong people" are not people pleasers.

But you may be surprised if I tell you that you may have a similar issue. With people-pleasers, either the fear of offense or the need for acceptance keeps them stuck in the "on" position. However, with strong people, it may not be recognized when one is constantly in the "on" position! Additionally, the need to produce creates the additional challenge of not knowing how to turn the production switch off.

Boundaries and Borders Are the Missing Keys

How can we guard our output and accessibility without telling people no all day? We do it by establishing and maintaining realistic borders and boundaries. Borders and boundaries are sometimes used synonymously but are defined differently and can have two separate applications.

The Oxford dictionary defines "boundary" as "A line that marks the limits of an area; a dividing line."[5] The word "border" is slightly different and determined by Merriam Webster as "an outer part or edge."[6] It may be difficult to see the difference between the two. For our discussion, borders define the outer edge or degree to which we participate or contribute to something. A border keeps us safe within a limited space. They are established by our human capacity and willingness to do or be something. Why is it so important to outline our borders? Because borders are more intended for us rather than for others around us. As previously mentioned, they keep us safe in a specified area. Convictions are borders. For example, you may have a conviction (character border) that establishes how you will participate in something appearing ungodly or lawless.

You may have a firm conviction on the concept of stealing, so much so that you would be compelled to return a change overage that a cashier may have given you in error. Others may take advantage of that oversight, but you don't overlook it to remain safe inside a clear conscious, which you have defined as righteous or good because of your clear character borders. This border is for you to stay in a specific space and is not necessary to keep you protected from the behavior of others.

Let's contrast this with a discussion on boundaries. A *boundary* is somewhat different in that it differentiates one area from another. It marks the end of the border of one place and the beginning of the border in another room or space. Boundaries are more for others. Well-set boundaries will communicate a specific location or area to which others do not have access unless you grant it. Just like borders, we all have boundaries. Boundaries keep others out of the spaces they should not occupy without your consent. One of the most familiar boundaries is called "personal space." Your personal space is the area around you considered private and comfortably belonging to you and activities such as speaking. This unique space differs with each person, and I know some people with incredibly short personal spaces, but I digress. However, everyone has this boundary. Once it is crossed, there is an awkwardness that you knowingly (sometimes unknowingly) autocorrect. You may back up or turn to the side; although different for everyone, there is some automatic indication to let the one that has crossed the boundary know that your personal space has been breached. If you stay in position once a person has crossed your space boundary, it signals your acceptance of their access to your space. Perhaps you may allow someone to lean in to give you a kiss or a hug; it means you have granted access to the area boundaries previously defined. Unless this personal space area is taken unwillingly or in a way that you have no control of, then it is up to you to define it so that you may guard it or grant access to it.

We need to know ourselves, the boundaries that are innately there, and the ones that need to be established. We must distinguish them so well that we autocorrect or mandate others to obey. Knowing when to back up, when to turn and reposition ourselves, or when to address the other party is crucial. To stay unchanged once a boundary has been crossed signals your permission and acceptance. Period.

Well-defined boundaries will keep others and us from having to guess about what should happen without consequence. Because boundaries establish your right to specific areas and are intended to keep you safe within and others formally in the place outside, there must always be a consequence or appropriate action when they are breached. On the other hand, if a boundary is not well defined to others, how can you enact a consequence?

> Others cannot breach a limit
> that you have not defined.

If you have not explained it, you have already allowed them permission to that area. That's substantial truth for anyone, including strong people.

Borders and Boundaries Are Not Just for Others to Follow

We must know that borders and boundaries are just as much for us to follow as it is for others. It's harder for us to slap ourselves on the wrist when we allow a break in our borders and boundaries. However, the consequences of broken borders/boundaries (B & B) have a way of finding us and providing the slap we did not give ourselves! As earlier mentioned, we have to resolve to say no to ourselves. When we experience burnout, it is usually not as much due to the inability to say no but rather the failure to set reasonable B & B and maintain them. The appropriate use of well-placed B & B can help solve issues within the scope of our output and accessibility and help protect our purpose from sabotage.

Outside of any illegal or coerced entry, access to you is a right that you must give. Whether that access is free or purchased is up to you. Your family and close friends may experience more of you because you have freely given access. Your employer or business contacts usually must pay to access you. Whatever method access is provided, it is considered your right to share. You must think of yourself as an area or sphere of great substance. You have a wealth of experience, knowledge, ability, influence, and even ambiance wrapped up within your sphere.

Get accustomed to screening those who can access you. You most likely already do that when you filter your phone calls. Limiting accessibility increases the respect of gaining accessibility. There should always be levels to your accessibility. Even when you buy a product service plan online, there are likely different tiers to that plan. The highest tier offers the highest level of access. If accessibility to you is obtainable at *any* level from anyone, there will be *no* respect of contact with you. But once there is a demand or cost to obtain a level of access to you, the respect level automatically goes up. There are parts of you that others must only have limited access to. Some people may have no access to you at all, especially if there has been a constant misuse or abuse of boundaries. This may be hard for some. But you will find that there is always someone to whom this must apply.

Suppose you find that people pile things on you (because it's so heavy for them), assuming that you can handle the weight and mental energy to take on their additional weight. At the time, they may not think of it as a weight to you, or maybe they just assume that you can handle it from the way you present yourself. The lack of management will expose your breaking point if you don't identify and manage your output.

> Without appropriate boundaries, multiple people can become too costly for you.

I know you want to help when it is in your power. But it must also be within your physical, mental, and emotional capacity at any given time.

There is a difference between taking something out of a sense of obligation or compassion and taking on something part of your current assignment. You should consult God as you ask yourself a question. Is this person or thing I am considering part of my assignment this hour and this season? If the answer from God is no, you must place the B & B's that communicate your unwillingness to participate in an activity or for them to have a level of access to you. It's not about being selfish. It's about being purposeful. Sometimes we may reason that a well-timed and crucial "no" is selfish, so we are uncertain what to communicate. But when you clarify how this request fits within your current assignment or overall purpose, the response of yes or no becomes clearer. This helps you eliminate those people, places, and things that are not providing a return on the investment of what you can provide. The return on investment will always be connected to your purpose. Each assignment is related to a purpose. If this person or thing is not part of an assignment, the answer mostly should be "no." Start by permitting yourself to say no to yourself, enabling you to say no to them. You are the responsible party for your borders and boundaries. Whether setting or maintaining the established limits, the buck stops with you.

One of my spiritual daughters noticed my lack of borders and boundaries regarding my time. I am a person who hates to "waste time." So much so that I found myself filling up my day from the moment I awoke until I went back to bed. Even while watching television, I would be thinking, *Is there something I need to be doing?* I would devalue quality downtime like watching a movie with the excuse of already seeing it once before. To watch it again was now wasting my time and keeping me from doing something else that needed my attention. She helped me understand that rest time is not wasted time. Even if I had seen the movie before, enjoy it again! Enjoy the cuddle time with my dearest friend, which is my husband. I needed a well-defined border to keep my mental well-being safe by establishing some stress-free "me time." Similarly, I needed time boundaries to keep others from taking up time that could be used for my much-needed downtime. One night she called and said we need to set up some office hours for you. Once office hours are over, you must know it is rest time. For my mental health, she let me know that I not only needed to say no to others who requested time from me after a specific time, but similarly, say no to myself to have time for refreshing and relaxing. At a specific time, I had to leave the "office" and go relax. I had to refrain from doing anything that required ministering, counseling, or any other mental expenditure that was not restful. By the time our conversation ended, I had a well-thought-out list of when my day would begin and end within the "office."

This concept of office hours would act as both a border and a boundary. I am forever grateful for my spiritual daughter, who saw that "room" in my house needing time management. Now, when others or I try to interfere with my rest time, I say, "My office hours are…" And it reminds me that I must rest to protect my physical and mental wellness.

Prayer

Father God, thank You for enlightening me regarding the value of what I supply to others. Thank You for allowing me to be a source others can access. I value this from You and thank You for the grace to manage my output and protect my access. Help me discern each situation so that I make the right decisions to keep what You've purposed me to do in a way that is effective and intact. In Jesus's name, I pray. Amen.

Wisdom Nugget

Manage your supply to others by establishing well-defined borders. Protect your access by setting well-defined boundaries. Do not breach your borders or allow others to breach your boundaries. Recognize the need to preserve and sustain yourself for the purposes established by God.

My Declaration

My output/production and my access are valuable. I manage my output and guard my access.

PROPHETIC LETTER:

I Will Send Help

Beloved,

I am your help! Just look to Me for help, and I will send it. It may not be in the form you thought when you cried out to Me. But it will always be the help I designed for you at the right time. I am your keeper, and as you stay in My secret place, I keep you under the shadow of My wings. I provide My help in time of your need. Do not fear; only look to Me. I always send Myself as help for My people. When My son Israel needed help, I sent Myself as Moses. When Moses needed help, I sent Myself as Jethro and Joshua. When Joshua needed help, I sent Myself as Rahab! If you have questions about who to trust, know My help will always represent Me! When you turn to Me, I will send you a form and reflection of Me. My heart, instruction, and desire for you will always be reflected in whom I send.

Only look for Me, and I will show you Myself. I will be for you a go-between; I will be for you a fortress, I will be for you a guide, I will be a comfort for you. I will be a provider, a healer, a counselor, and a friend. What area of your life is outside of My sight? What issue is too complex for Me to deliver? Know that I will never leave you without help. I will send My help by sending a reflection of Myself. Look for My reflection in the ones I send. My grace will always be appropriate for My purposes. My purpose for you will always be made open. My mercy will always be extended. Only look to Me, and I will send Myself as a help for you.

CHAPTER 5:

Know Your Source of Strength

I will lift up mine eyes unto the hills, from whence
cometh my help. My help cometh from the LORD,
which made heaven and earth. He will not suffer thy
foot to be moved: he that keepeth thee will not slumber.
Behold, he that keepeth Israel shall neither slumber
nor sleep. The LORD is thy keeper: the LORD is thy
shade upon thy right hand. The sun shall not smite
thee by day, nor the moon by night. The LORD shall
preserve thee from all evil: he shall preserve thy soul.
The LORD shall preserve thy going out and thy coming
in from this time forth, and even forevermore.

—Psalm 121 (KJV)

I remember an occurrence that happened to me in my late twenties or early thirties when I traveled to New York for an event with my former spouse. After getting him to the prepping area for a performance, I had to return to the hotel to get dressed for the performance that night. I know I'm aging myself, but this was before the days of navigation systems. I had my trusty paper map. I paid attention to how he got to the building, and it seemed like a straight shot to get back to our hotel. Was I wrong! It was not because I didn't have a good memory; instead, I was not experienced with New York City traffic and how to maneuver within this extremely fast-paced transportation system. It was uncanny how much I was *not* in control of even simple turns and lane changes. The traffic carried me to places that I did not want to go! After a while, I realized I was lost.

I maneuvered to a side street and asked for directions: "Please, ma'am, do you know how I can get to my hotel [I forgot the name]?"

The response was, "Yeah, sure. *All you have to do is* go two blocks down this street; then you're *going to* make a right at the third light and then take the third exit on the right, which puts you on the main highway. Then you just follow that highway and get off at the fifth exit. Turn onto the main street, and the hotel is on the right—*you can't miss it.*"

It seemed simple to me! So, I started again, and as before, the traffic carried me to places I did not want to go. I had to stop for directions again; this time, it was a gentleman. He instructed me on finding my hotel, starting with those famous New-Yorker words *"all you have to do is"* and ending with the even more annoying line of *"you can't miss it."* Well, I *did* miss it!

Again and again, I asked for directions, and again and again, I missed it! In desperation and frustration, I cried out to God, "Please help me, God! I don't know what to do."

I took the first exit that traffic allowed me to take and stopped at a mall. I went inside the first store I could get to and proceeded to ask if there was a way to find a police officer. Indeed, a police officer would find a way to get me back to my hotel. Tracking down the first person who would listen to me, I told my story. Well, you may already know what sentence they started with: "All you have to do is […] you can't miss it"!

I broke down and was in tears as I screamed, "*Yes, I can miss it*, and *I assure you, I will miss it!* I don't need any more directions; *I need someone* to help me. I need someone to lead me."

A gentleman that overheard my story and saw my desperation and utter lack of composure offered to escort me to my destination. I accepted his help and pleaded with him to drive slowly and don't lose me. He said, "I won't lose you!" He did end up getting me to the hotel, and I could not be more thankful to him. I knew God was with me through the help He sent me. God is everywhere, and that day, the gentleman that helped me was a reflection of God not leaving me or losing me when things looked hopeless. We know that God is always our help. But there are times that we need human physical help. I cried out to God, and God responded with a human physical resource!

Who Is Your Help?

Who would you say is your source of strength? Most of us would say God…and *He* is our help. But God is really promising help "from" Him. God always sends aid; He wants to send help! As Psalm 121 says, our help comes *from* the Lord. As reflected in my true story above, the support God sends is not always mystical and supernatural. Most of the time, God sends everyday people to help us! When we look to the Lord, there will be help. The Lord will send the help! God will send to you that which reflects His love toward you and His help to you. This will mostly be in the form of people.

God does use angels as well. Angels ministered to Jesus, Elijah, etc. Although the Bible says we can entertain angels unaware, it's most likely not an angel that will be that source of strength to you. You *are* strong, but you also need someone or something that can help you refuel, reset, restore, and just be *more* complete.

Sometimes, we must be settled and grounded in our thoughts or feelings.

> Everyone needs someone else! As a strong person, you need help just as much as others to which you may provide help.

It may not be in areas of your strength; however, you need assistance from others simply because you are a human with human needs that cannot be fulfilled by you alone. You have heard that no man is an island. You must acknowledge that you are not an island. You will not survive alone. In a world where it may be hard for you to trust anyone, even the closest of family members, it can put an enormous strain on our trust level that God's help in the form of people is needed and supplied for us. When you have found that friend, that confidant, sometimes you may doubt if they are the appropriate help for you at that specific time of your life. It can, undoubtedly, be difficult to find someone in your circle who resonances with God's promise of support. However, we know that scripture assures us that help will come from Him as we look to Him. The key word in that statement is "from." God assures us that aid will be sent.

There is no limitation on God. He is the one that created the heavens and the earth. There will be nothing that can hinder him from sending help. There can be no force in the heavens or the earth that can stop Him. Not even will God restrict Himself, for He speaks in this psalm that He does not even have a sleep limitation that could prevent or delay Him from being a keeper for you. In this expression of His word, "keeper" means one who is to "keep," "preserve," "protect," and "attend to" (directed toward a person). Nothing will stop or slow Him from safeguarding, watching, and listening to you and the purpose He created for you to complete.

So, how do we identify those who God has sent to help us? They will always be in His reflection. Those He sends to preserve, protect, and attend to us, and the purpose He has created in us will be a reflection of God Himself. There cannot be protection and preservation from those that are jealous, openly or secretly resentful of you, or either a direct or indirect sabotage of you or your purpose. God is not jealous or envious of you. He does not strive against you or take control of you so He can look good. Think of the attributes of God as you consider those sent to help you.

Please understand that I am not saying it will always be a sweet "Yes, man"! It may be a person who will not only tell you what you want to hear but what you need to hear. They will reflect who God is by how much we flourish and grow from what they provide. We must not discount that type of person in our lives.

Recognize the People Positioned to be a Source for You

Identifying your source(s) and knowing how to depend on and receive from the resources they provide is essential. Have you considered your most consistent and trustworthy source of support and strength? What or who is it? My husband is the primary person I trust to provide sustenance and support in my life. One reason I can lean on him for strength is he does not control or battle against who I am as a person or my abilities. If you have a spouse or friend who opposes or refuses to recognize your purpose or strengths, it will be challenging for you to lean on them for support. My first marriage was a constant fight to maintain who I was simply because of his inability to support a strong person as a wife. I do not have a strong personality. I have never been a "my way or the highway" type. But there was intimidation and an expectancy to crouch or dummy down to accommodate his ego. I did exactly that! So, I know how to do that, and most strong people have learned to do this to a certain degree as we cope with the sensitivities or egos of others.

> We may want to make others feel comfortable with the strength we possess.
> But realize there will be those who will never be satisfied with your strengths.
> Even those that you serve and love.

It's very hurtful to provide services to someone who needs and resents you simultaneously, but unfortunately, this is the predicament in which strong people (namely strong women) find themselves.

While I have learned that I must manage myself, I also learned to rely on my husband as a primary source to help me with how to accomplish that. I manage myself, but I yield to the safety of his counsel and the protection it brings. I understand I must uncover those vulnerable areas to the covering of his love to preserve my mental and emotional health. When God sent my second (and final) husband, He sent a reflection of Himself. It was not about the outward, as God revealed Himself in my husband's heart and how he cared for me, which included my purpose in God. There was no intimidation. We quickly deal with issues whenever there is an opportunity for opposition or pressure because we know who we are married to. We support each other as he also has a strong call from God in his life. We realize the importance of our ministries, and neither is one-sided.

Position Yourself to Receive from Your Sources

How do we receive from those God sends as help? Firstly, we acknowledge our need to obtain the help (reflection of God) that God sends. It is futile to pray for the Lord's help and then refuse to receive from them once God establishes them for us. No one is perfect, but that is why we need each other. You will most likely identify flaws in the sources that God sends. Rather than focusing on the flaws, pinpoint the areas you can glean from. The areas to which God's designed help can pour into you will nourish you in your present state and support you in the next God-ordained assignment of your life. Secondly, we must recognize their contributions to those areas we need support. Communicate with them and let them know you are open to receiving what they provide for you. If God sent them, they are necessary for your life. Make them aware of that. Trust what they contribute to you. Make it a valuable investment for them by receiving what they contribute. Lastly, we must deal with and remove any barriers that keep us in a state of resistance and self-reliance. As we commit to supporting this process of receiving open and healthy, we will see the wholeness God intended when He sent them to our aid.

Prayer

Father God, I love You and who You are to me. Thank You for sending reflections of that love to me to aid me in the purpose You created me for. Thank You for the grace that allows me to receive the people You send to me. Thank You for helping me glean from them, knowing I can trust them, as You purposed them to help me. In Jesus's name, I pray. Amen.

Wisdom Nugget

Although independent and knowledgeable, avoid rejecting the help that God sends to you through other people. Understand that when God sends you aid, it will reflect Him. Therefore, when people provide unholy and dishonorable assistance, you can discern this is not from the Lord.

My Declaration

I look to the Lord for help and receive His help through the people sent, the reflections of my heavenly Father.

PROPHETIC LETTER:

See as I See

Beloved,

I am Jehovah Roi, the One who sees. I see you as the creation I made. I also see your adversary, for he was also created. The enemy knows that I see everything within his arsenal. He expects that you don't see the same way I see. But I have placed My Spirit inside you so that you may see how I see, so that you may discern the enemy's presence and his tactics. For the weapons of your warfare are mighty through My Spirit within you. Now see as I see. Command as I command. My words have been hidden in your heart so that you may release My words.

I have not only given you physical eyes but also spiritual eyes. Your eyesight sharpens to My will and My ways as you spend time with Me. Words that shape your purpose come forth based on how well you see as I see. Get in sync with Me, and I will cause you to operate in the authority I have ordered and released. The enemy does not have the power you imagine he has when you see as I see. I see the devices he uses to weaken you, but the authority I have given you will render his devices ineffective. But you must first see as I see. Open your eyes and see what I have placed before you. It is a great expanse of purpose and gifting, but you must see that it is inside you. Open the eyes of your spirit and see yourself as I see you, for then you will be strong and courageous to complete everything assigned to your life. I am faithful in My assignment for you. See My faithfulness as a sign that you can meet all My hand has established. Beloved, see as I see.

CHAPTER 6:

Recognize Sabotage

For this is why I wrote that I might test you and know whether you are obedient in everything. Anyone whom you forgive, I also forgive. Indeed, what I have forgiven, if I have forgiven anything, has been for your sake in the presence of Christ, so that we would not be outwitted by Satan; for we are not ignorant of his designs.

—2 Corinthians 2:9–11 (ESV)

L ife can knock holes in any armor. No matter how many boundaries and borders we establish, life can find a way inside.

Our physical bodies, our soul (mind, will, and emotions), and our spirit-man all need the ability to withstand the pressures and forces we will inevitably face in life. This substance of "strength" is necessary for every compartment of life. Physical strength is fantastic but can fail us. Our soul is constantly experiencing both the pleasures and pressures of life and has the propensity to get overwhelmed. Our physical strength relies on the strength of our inner man, called our spirit. If our inner man operates continuously without the rest, renewal, and restoration from the spirit of God, then a meltdown of our physical strength is very likely. The strength of our inner man is what keeps us going, even when there is an extreme lack of physical strength. Strong people need to grasp the importance of maintaining their inner strength.

> The anointing, gifts, talents, titles, and positions are excellent and essential in our assignments. Still, the strength of our inner man is ultimately what supports us as the people behind our purposes.

The enemy sabotages the power of our inner man by attacking those areas that are weak, not well managed, and frail from spiritual malnutrition and neglect.

The enemy knows how to poke holes in our inner man to siphon the strength of our inner man. He will use sabotaging enemies like fear, anger, grief, discouragement, rejection, trauma, etc. Sometimes these saboteurs can appear subtle, but it will become apparent that sabotage has taken place as we awaken and start to wonder what happened to our strength? Not just physical strength, but our inner strength. Let's realize the enemy does not fight fair or passively. He is very aggressive with his tactics. When the inner man's strength is down, the enemy will bring on the most brutal attacks in places he knows will cause trauma and make us want to give up. The episodes are geared to making you want to give up on life, give up on the promises of God, give up on your beliefs—just give up, period!

Ephesians 6:13 (ESV) lets us know that for our inner man to stand against enemy sabotage, we must "therefore; take up the whole armor of God, that you may be able to withstand in the evil day, and having done all, to stand firm." We will have done all we can to stand when we do this. *And* because God is our source of all of the armor, we *shall* stand firm! Most importantly, we will know that our inner strength comes directly from our creator—God!

The Armor of God that fortifies and protects our inner man include:

The Belt of Truth
(the Truth of God's Word)

We must read His Word, meditate on His Word, and pray His Word. Gaining every nutrient from the *logos*, or written word, and depending on Holy Spirit to cause it to become the *rhema*, or revealed word, of God. Once we have a revelation of the Word, it becomes alive to us. It then belongs to us and builds our faith in the power of God through whatever He has revealed.

The Breastplate of
Righteousness

We know this is the imputed righteousness of Christ. We are never righteous within ourselves. But we must submit under and take on the righteousness of Christ. We need His righteousness placed on us because part of the enemy's schemes uses actual spiritual legalities. The devil is an accuser of the people of God, and he will bring accusations against us. If those accusations are correct, we can actually be charged and penalized legally according to the Word of God.

*For when you are going with your accuser to appear
before the magistrate [God the Judge], on the way,
make an effort to settle with him [Repent and come
under the imputed righteousness of Christ] so that he
[the enemy] does not drag you before the judge, and the
judge hand you over to the officer [the legal system in
heaven], and the officer throw you into prison [cap-
tivity]. I tell you, you will not get out of there until
you have paid up the very last lepton [made complete
recompense for the wrongs done].*

—Luke 12:58–59 (NASB);
text in brackets mine

This verse lets us know there are legalities in the heavenly realm and there is judgment and penance. Although God is the judge and magistrate, He must uphold the righteousness of His word. If there is an accusation that is true against you, you are held liable. However, because Christ took the penalty for our sin, then when we impute our sins under the due penalty that has already been paid by Christ, then we can become righteous in God by His Son Jesus Christ.

The Helmet of Salvation

The Lord has made provision for our protection and resistance against enemy impact. We are protecting our minds from illusion, ignorance, danger, or even failure. God is the author of our salvation (deliverance). When we renew our minds with the Word of God, revelation (from God and others), mentorship, training/instruction, wisdom, and consistent time in the presence of God; then we protect the strength of our inner man and guard against attempted sabotage from the enemy against our mind, will, and emotions.

The Shield of Faith

Faith is a force that comes from deep inside each man. We have been given a measure of faith from God. Our faith has to be built up by the renewing of our minds. Romans 10:17 (KJV) says, "So then faith cometh by hearing [...]" (not physical hearing)—if it were physical hearing, the next verse of this scripture would not say, "and hearing by the word of God." The hearing that is described in this scripture is revelatory hearing. As we read the Word of God, His supernatural revelation becomes alive and strengthens the supernatural substance of faith. Faith is born from revelation or hearing in our inner man. Then our faith grows stronger by staying in the presence and practicing the things of God, like prayer. "But you, beloved, building yourselves up in your most holy faith and praying in the Holy Spirit" (Jude 1:20, ESV).

Shoes of the Gospel of Peace

Faith comes from revelation or hearing in our inner man. That word "peace" is *shalom*, or "wholeness." Isaiah 55:3 tells us that the chastisement of our peace was upon Him (Christ), which means the punishment or judgment against our peace (wholeness) was laid upon Christ. This peace is not just mental or emotional peace but refers to our wholeness in every area. We are redeemed back to God and the state of wholeness that only comes from and through God. Christ took the punishment for sin that fights against our wholeness and paid it off entirely and legally! We, therefore, stand under the propitiation of His finished work and take the good news (gospel) of wholeness in our inner man. We can defend ourselves against the wiles and attacks of the devil by declaring and standing firmly on our wholeness (peace) as paid in full by Christ.

Sword of the Spirit

The sword of the spirit and the helmet of salvation both connect in Scripture to the word of God. As the helmet is defensively required to protect against attacks from the enemy, the sword is offensively required to be used against the enemy. Jesus used Scripture offensively when Satan tempted Him in the wilderness. The enemy could not legally counter his offensive stance with the word of God, as Satan knows the power of the word of God and legally what he can do within the legal confines of God's word. This is why our ignorance of the Word of God can be destructive to us and advantageous to the enemy. Hosea 4:6 (KJV) declares, "My people are destroyed for lack of knowledge [...]."

Use the Word of God, Scripture, consistently and effectively against the enemy. The enemy (diabolical forces) must submit to the *consistent, effective* use of the Word God!

The nourishment needed for the building up and guarding of our inner man can only come from the revelation and renewal produced from the reading of the Word of God, meditation, prayer, repentance, submission under the righteousness of the finished work of Christ (breastplate of righteousness), godly counsel and wisdom (from God and others) from mentorship, training, and instruction, and indeed, most importantly, consistent time in the presence of God.

There will be opposition: the enemy *always* has a plan (strategy) and a reason for every attack against you. It's not a random afterthought by the enemy when you are in heavy opposition. Indeed, Satan does not like you, but it's more about what's inside you and your *threat* to his plan. There is always strategy/plans and purpose to every attack from Satan. In our scripture, we read a lot regarding war over physical land. In the spirit, the "land" is your God-given purpose, so the enemy fights you to conquer the land, or what's inside you. The enemy's desired possession is not your car, job, house, etc., although he will use that. But it's deeper. It is a more profound plan of stealing your strength to the point that you would be so discouraged that you would abandon your purpose. If we don't recognize the purpose for which the enemy is fighting us, we get lost in our feelings and the smoke screens the enemy throws at us, which affects how we handle and overcome the opposition.

But the Bible clarifies that we should be aware of his diabolical devices. We should recognize the sabotage and ultimately do something more than just talk about it. There is an innate desire to surround ourselves with those who will empathize with our problem, which only brings temporary emotional relief. The godly counsel goes past allowing you to vent and offers a strategy for your victory against enemy havoc.

The most unpleasant part of discovering who our enemies are is examining who we are! Understanding who we are *and* being honest with who we see in the mirror. This self-reflection will help us see our enemies and the triggers he uses against us. We can't keep blaming everyone else when we fall for the same provocations. Know your triggers and formulate your strategy for dealing with them. Suppose you shut down and respond negatively or angrily when things are considered offensive to you. In that case, the enemy will supply you with plenty of hurtful or insulting statements or at least perceived by you as such. The response to offense is defense. If you have been told that you are often very defensive, you most likely take offense easier than others. The perpetuating factor with an offensive nature is that you will most likely defend yourself to the degree that you deny there is an issue or that you are easily offended. An offensive spirit is pervasive and usually comes from being deeply hurt, usually by someone very close and, at some point, trusted. Who would want to go and revisit something or someone that hurt them immensely? However, with godly help, we can revisit the hurtful past and be released from the prison of bondage to offense.

It is the enemy's strategy to destroy you, and if he can do that from within and with your help, it is to his advantage. "Be sober, be vigilant; because your adversary the devil, as a roaring lion, walketh about, seeking whom he may devour" (1 Peter 5:8, KJV).

Knowing how the enemy works against you is crucial. There are schemes used that are specifically tailored to you. The Bible states we should not be ignorant of his devices so Satan will not have an advantage over us. In addition to the spirit of offense, numerous spirits can sabotage our inner man's health. Satan uses these spiritual forces often because they can be effective against strong men and women.

There are many saboteurs of strong people. In this book, I will only cover three common ones. The three significant forces can be directed toward you with the assignment to shut down the purposes God placed in you, which is to be a strength or supply toward others.

Common Sabotaging Forces Include

Rejection

"To reject" means "to refuse to accept, consider, submit to, take for some purpose, or use"; "to refuse to hear, receive, or admit." [7]

People who are rejected feel unwanted and substandard to a desired person or thing. Even as a leader today, rejection is a sabotaging spirit that will trigger a reaction within me that I have to recognize and lean on Holy Spirit to help me. I struggle most when it is a rejection of the knowledge I desire to pour out and impart. I mentor so that others don't have to go through the same things that I did. I create solutions so that others don't have to go through the pain I experienced. Some people receive and prosper, and some don't and resent me and the wisdom I try to provide.

As a teacher, I am passionate about passing on knowledge and insight. I wished more people would grab it. I pour in with passion; therefore, when I would feel even the most minor level of rejection, I tended to drop all further aid. Of course, this is different with my children, as I will never give up on them. However, with those who I pour into and mentor, it was a weakness I had to recognize as a sabotage of the very purpose I was created for, which is to pour into or mentor others. Of course, I had all the right words to support my actions, and to a certain extent, they were true. I would say it's okay to return their rejection with my rejection of them because they did not value my investment in them. I was guilty of employing the same spirit sent to deter me, to use my displeasure against those I felt deserved my wrath. I had to recognize this as a trigger for me. It was an issue I had to overcome and still have to guard against. As a mentor, coach, or just a spiritual authority figure, it is important not to drop the people assigned to me. I had to realize this spirit of rejection sabotaged my purpose if I allowed it to accomplish its assignment of stopping me from the very purpose for which I was placed on the earth. In addition, those assigned to me also went unfulfilled and were most likely to mistrust future authority figures. I'm not saying we should continue to pour out and drain ourselves to those that don't value what we have to offer. I'm simply saying that I had to evaluate each situation based on its merit and not let the actual or perceived rejection cause me to act in a retaliatory manner. Some cases call for unwavering love and patience to breakthrough issues that one may face, while other conditions call for boundaries to be set in order. Realize that some people who say you "dropped them" wiggled free from your help. It was ultimately their responsibility to receive.

For example, I have experienced poverty and the utter despair of not being able to provide for my children or myself. I have been in situations of not having money to buy bare necessities for my family, like food for a meal. Because of that pain, I came up with some creative solutions that have served me well over the years. I have gone from the financial struggle with bad credit and all the hardships that can come with a bad credit score. I learned some things and was able to go from a score in the low 600s to one that is now close to 850 (the highest FICO score possible). So, when I see people struggle financially, I want to provide immediate assistance with cash but also with knowledge. There is robust wisdom and instruction that I long to deliver so that person can experience the freedom I now enjoy. I realize money is a sensitive topic, and if you are in need, the last thing you want is someone's advice. But when the time is right, I offer suggestions anyway. I have seen that when the direction and instructions are received, the recipients increase their chances of never falling into bad financial situations again. However, there have also been scenarios where it was clear the only thing desired was consistent handouts and not a hand-up. This type of setting called for quick and consistent boundaries on my part so that I was not drained by someone that took advantage of my compassion. There was a need to remain consistent in my set limits, even when their sad story became sadder. A proper attitude of wanting help would also include receiving instruction and wisdom. When it is obvious the recipient only wants a handout with no desire to take the responsibility of change, I have learned to leave people in an undesired state and not feel guilty.

> You are different by design! And rejection usually comes because of your difference.

Realize you are to do great things with what God has proposed. But grasp this truth: you will only complete *your* purpose when you operate in *your* difference! If you operate the same way everyone else does, it may create comfort, but working in sameness will not produce the effect you were created to do. Never fret when others reject your difference because it's your difference that makes you valuable. You will *never* experience the satisfaction of being renowned without first experiencing the rejection of being *different!*

What is your strategy against *rejection*?

- Understand rejection comes because of your incredible difference! Sameness will never trigger rejection from others. Some people will reject the difference in you.
- Own and constantly celebrate your difference. This will help protect you from the mind games you experience when others reject you.
- Recognize past rejection wounds and seek the help needed to recover.
- *Forgive* those who have rejected you.
- Ask God for an additional strategy to counter this spirit in your specific situation.

Intimidation

The word means "to make timid or fearful." [8]

Some people skillfully use intimidation to frighten or threaten others to submit or accept their will or elicit a feeling of inferiority in others so that their power takes precedence in the minds of others. But there is also an utterly involuntary intimidation reaction you can evoke in others simply by walking in the strength of your purpose.

> When you are strong, people will be intimidated by you and your power even if you have no clue that you are an intimidating figure.

"The Strong One": Godly Wisdom for the Person Behind the Purpose

This is especially true if you are dealing with insecure personalities.

I did a lot of my younger life alone. People either liked me or did not like me at all! It took me a long time to realize an intimidation factor was involved in most cases. It is human nature for people to compare themselves to others. I have learned that people will respond to you in how you make them feel about themselves in comparison to you. This is not as easy as it sounds because we tend to leave out the part about "in comparison to you." For example, you can give compliments and tributes to others on their ideas or accomplishments until the cows come home; but if *their perspective* regarding their victory does not meet or exceed what they perceive as your accomplishment(s), it may make them feel inferior to you; thus, making it a good possibility they may not "like" you. Not because of what you say about or to them, but how you make them feel about themselves when they are around you. In contrast, if you achieved something perceived as mediocre or able to be surpassed by them, it can make them more comfortable being around you, as they feel better about themselves when they are around you. Constant comparison breeds a level of insecurity the enemy will use to trap us outside our awareness or it. You may feel you have to accommodate for their lack or risk losing their support, friendship, or relationship (even family). You have a choice. Do you face the resentment, intimidation, comparison, and competition that may continue to present itself, or do you come down to the level where you feel you are more "acceptable" to them? It takes courage not to come down.

As I did for years, you can use this as a pain point. I tried to make people understand how everyone was wired differently.

I even did personality discovery and awareness workshops hoping everyone would come to see and like the real me on the inside and that I was not a threat to them. The personality workshops failed as they reinforced some people to find more reasons why they should not like the people they already disliked. I was stunned. I discovered I had to own my insecurity about being "different" and authentically me. It was not about making others understand me more than accepting and loving my difference with or without approval from others. Insecurity and intimidation will always be a part of human nature; therefore, I challenge you to move into a state of being comfortable when you are misunderstood. As long as you are authentic in who God created you, walk freely in purpose even when confronted with this type of sabotage.

What is your strategy against *intimidation*?

- Recognize how you respond when faced with intimidation.
- Understand, accept, and love who you are in the will and purposes of God.
- Find what keeps you encouraged in the face of people who may be intimidated by your strength (positive affirmations, support from your sources of strength, etc.).
- Keep your purpose moving.
- *Forgive* those intimidated by you.
- Ask God for an additional strategy to counter this spirit in your specific situation.

Offense

"Offense" is "the act of displeasing or affronting" or "the state of being insulted or morally outraged." [9]

This is a complex spirit to maneuver against. I find the main reason this spirit is so eluding is that there is always a defense of it by the one under its influence.

It is also one of the easiest spirits to discern, as defense is the opposite reaction of offense. Therefore, those under the influence of offense commonly respond to things regarding themselves with defensive statements. Sometimes outlandish defensive statements and sometimes very subtle. Do you often hear, "You tend to be very defensive"? If so, you may be dealing with a spirit of offense. You may have even tried to make your defensive statements more subtle to counter this observation from others. However, making your defensive response more subtle does not deal with the underlying spiritual force of offense. You may know someone under the influence of a spirit of offense and have learned to either "walk on eggshells" around them by avoiding certain subjects, word choices, or even facial expressions. It's never easy, as an offense can be taken in the most innocent circumstances. Avoidance does not help much when dealing with those influenced by this spirit.

When someone takes offense, thoughts from the perceived offense can spiral to the point where they destroy the person internally. It is a powerful spirit that commonly works against those in authority. Another characteristic to recognize about someone under the influence of this spirit is the inability to forgive quickly. A trauma that could not easily be forgiven is often the doorway in which this spirit takes a foothold. Forgive often and promptly. Countering and deliverance from this spirit calls for prayer and fasting, as counsel is usually ineffective without prayer.

It is prevalent for a solid person to continuously encounter those under the influence of offense or be under a heavy offense influence themselves. Therefore, this spirit can sabotage and cause you to self-sabotage your purpose if not dealt with.

What is your strategy against *the spirit of offense*?

- Recognize when someone is under the influence of a spirit of offense.
- Command the enemy to remove the blinders and pray for the supernatural insight to be revealed to the person under the influence of a spirit of offense.
- Ask God for an additional strategy to counter this spirit in your specific situation.
- Understand the importance of forgiveness, as this is a primary starting point for an offensive spirit. *Forgive* those that offend you and those offended by the authentic you.
- If you find that you are under a heavy influence of offensive, ask for forgiveness and the grace of God to help you forgive quickly.

Prayer

Father God, thank You for calling me an overcomer. Through your Word, I have authority over serpents and scorpions and over *all* the power of the enemy. Thank You, as I recognize I am already victorious through Your Word. My purpose prevails because Your Word prevails. Provide the insight and discernment I need to acknowledge every enemy device and counter them victoriously. In Jesus's name, I pray. Amen.

Wisdom Nugget

Understand that opposition will come. Acknowledge and recognize feelings of rejection, unworthiness, negative thoughts, or fear that come to overwhelm you. Glean from the wisdom and mentorship that God has placed around you. Do not respond negatively or retreat in the face of opposition, understanding that with influence comes opposition. Understand when you see resistance, it may be a sign that you are doing precisely what you have been called to do. Stay focused, remain in a position to receive God's strategies against opposition, and keep your head up. Reject destructive criticism and forgive quickly. Receive the grace of God to forgive when you cannot do so.

My Declaration

Through the help of the Lord, I have the wisdom, authority, and strategies to overcome all opposition from the enemy.

PROPHETIC LETTER:
Trust Me

Beloved,

When you hurt, trust Me. I am the strong tower that protects and shelters you. I am your fortress of strength, the place where you can heal from the inside. Speak with Me, and I will speak with you. Lean on Me when the hurt seems overwhelming. I won't allow it to overtake you. I know how to restore you, just release yourself to Me. Realize your need for Me and rest on Me. I will be your hope when hope has been stripped from you.

You will know that you trust Me when you can release the things that have hurt you into My care and love for you. You must know that I love you, and I only can deliver you from the hurt. Only by My Spirit can your inner man be restored. Trust Me with the very men that try to damage and demolish you. Trust that I see the intents of the heart of men, and I know how to turn it for My glory to be revealed in you. I am Jehovah Shammah, and I'm already there on the other side of the pain, the grief, and the hurt. I see when others are there to harm you, and I diminish the effect of every weapon. If you feel the pain caused by the wounds, know that My intent for your good shall prevail. All the hurt works together to complete you in My plan. Trust Me with your heart so I can heal the pain that tries to scar and harden it. I need your heart to remain soft to My voice. I need your hands lifted as you cast every care into My hands. I need your feet to swiftly run in the direction I send you and not in the direction of retreat from the pain. Because I have ordered every step and every turn, you can trust Me in My purposed will for your life. My beloved, if you will only trust Me, I will get you to the other side. Trust Me.

CHAPTER 7:

Strong People Hurt Too

*The Lord is my shepherd, I will not be in need. He
lets me lie down in green pastures; He leads me beside
quiet waters. He restores my soul; He guides me in
the paths of righteousness for the sake of His name.
Even though I walk through the valley of the shadow
of death, I fear no evil, for You are with me; Your
rod and Your staff, they comfort me. You prepare a
table before me in the presence of my enemies; You
have anointed my head with oil; My cup overflows.
Certainly goodness and faithfulness will follow me
all the days of my life, and my dwelling will be in the
house of the Lord forever.*

—Psalm 23 (NASB)

Everyone experiences hurt. It is unavoidable. Usually, people do not walk toward hurt; they run away. But it is brokenness and pain that have made you who you are. Strength comes to you at a cost. Pain is a price tag for strength. Your strength does not make you immune to pain, even if others perceive that to be true.

Why Is the Pain Different with You?

Be aware that being strong doesn't mean you are always right. Sometimes people react to you negatively or may even reject you because of undesirable behavior or actions that you show. Rejection in any form can hurt. But when we are rejected due to our bad behavior, we should look inwardly and find a way to change the behavior. Rejection is not always because someone else cannot handle us! Sometimes, it is because we do need to change! You are vital for a reason, and natural strength always involves an insider look from you into you. But how do you handle the rejection that *will* come not because of adverse behaviors on your part but simply because of your strengths? This form of rejection is mainly due to intimidation. Rejection due to intimidation is still a rejection, and it still hurts.

It is hurtful to be rejected because of your strengths. Sometimes it's because people see how strong you are in that area and conclude that you will get over it faster than someone else could. Maybe you take things quieter than others. People will look at you and see you as being able to "take a licking and keep on ticking." Another phrase you may hear is I took on more concern for others in various situations because I saw you as the "bigger person." People recognize you can handle challenging situations well.

> Being seen as the one who can always absorb the punch may explain why you are taking more punches than others.

My husband and I took care of my parents during their senior years before they passed. My parents passed away within two months of each other, and the year of their deaths was one of the most trying and emotionally draining periods of my life. My dad passed first, and during his funeral, I was the one that took responsibility for all the activities surrounding the burial arrangements. My husband and I took care of everything others would not or could not. When parts of the family got into town, attitudes showed in some areas. Not that they were not given a chance to be included. Everyone had opinions. Some chose not to take responsibility for doing the work necessary for what they desired. And some thought certain things were unnecessary, so they did not want to be included in its planning. There were subsequently bitter feelings when things were performed without their cooperation. There were noticeable reactions when it was realized that things would go on without their involvement or input. The funeral director saw all the difficult family dynamics. Once the family arrived at the funeral and burial ceremonies, the attitudes were so apparent that the funeral director decided to make certain acknowledgments and presentations to a disgruntled family member. When I looked his way, he motioned and whispered to me, "I knew that you were the strong one and could take things better than the others. Therefore, I knew you would not mind if I accommodated those who appeared unhappy so they would not make a scene or feel left out."

At that time, it was okay because it did help to squelch high emotions. However, once things were over and the dust settled, I realized how discriminating this action was because it was based on the rationale that my strength kept me from feeling in the moment. In reality, I was intensely hurting during the whole time. I may not have looked as if I was about to break, but I was emotionally drained and wounded inwardly. Because of the strength others saw, specific actions were taken because the perception was I could handle things better. So, I absorbed the punches, but it didn't mean I didn't feel the sting of those punches, especially later during the quiet times of the night. It was as if I was being penalized for being the strong one.

This perception continues to happen. I knew I had to manage and not just handle those life moments when it hurt being strong.

Expectations Continue, Even When You Are in Pain

You may have figured out that other people expect more from you, even in extreme pain. This is especially true if you are a leader. It may be because the level of pain you feel may not show outwardly as it does in others. You do not intentionally do this, but it may be just a part of being you. It is likely because others expect you to handle anything that comes to you. It may be because some people are naturally selfish and don't want to see the level of pain you may be in. Then other times, people just don't expect you to hurt at all. It lends to the feelings or questions you may have of how you manage to keep getting into the same scenario where you seem to take care of everyone else, but when you are in need, you hurt alone. Why can't others see that you may need them just as they need you? How do you stop the emotional bleeding you sometimes fail to recognize? How do you stop the expectation cycle from others and remain true to yourself and your purpose? These and other questions must be asked by you so that you can break or manage the expectation cycle that has formed based on your strengths.

How Do I Stop the Bleeding When I Experience Hurt?

Sometimes we need healing in our spirit! We all bleed at some moments in life. When we bleed, we discharge or lose blood from a cut or wound. This blood flow can be released inside (internal bleed) or outside (external bleed). Similarly, there are "bleeding" processes when an emotional cut or injury occurs. Just as blood represents life, an emotional bleed causes us to lose life (blood) from places where it is meant to sustain us, whether they are internal or external. We cannot stay in an area of constant life loss. The hemorrhaging of peace from wounds of hurt, rejection, mistreatment, loss, etc., must be dealt with. These wounds take place deep within, and we may not be aware of the extent of the inside assault right away. But once we notice it, some decisions are needed to expose the source of the injury (what caused it?) and help stop the spread and further assault. Just as a physical bruise may take time before you see it, spiritual bruises may take a little time after the onslaught or injury before we feel and see them.

God is our refuge, a place of comfort as He applies gentle but direct pressure against our wounds to stop the bleeding and restore us to purpose. He renews our spirit as He leads us to the green pastures of restoration. When we remain in a state of vulnerability and openness to God, He, in turn, will reveal where He wants to stop the bleeding and restore us from the wounded areas. As we expressed earlier, God will also supply those around us that can help us.

"But I will restore you to health and heal your wounds,' declares the ^{Lord} [...]"

—Jeremiah 30:17 (NIV)

Restore to me the joy of your salvation, and uphold me with a willing spirit.

—Psalm 51:12 (ESV)

Why You Must Manage Expectations from Others

I challenge you to examine and then manage the expectations placed on you by those around you. If we fail to address the expectations efficiently and effectively from those around us, those expectations will eventually overgrow and overwhelm us, leading to stress, anxiety, and burnout. Like an unmanaged garden, order never grows on its own, only chaos. When first planted, gardens are beautiful. But if it is not managed, weeds take over, the intended plants wither or die, bugs and other animals invade, and it can take tremendous energy to get things back under control. The opposite of organization (to put in order) is disorder. Remember, unmanaged things do not grow toward organization; instead, they grow toward anarchy. The same thing happens when you and the expectations from others are not well managed. The relationship between you and the heavy or unrealistic expectations can lead to overwhelming physical and emotional disorder.

One way to alter the expectation cycle is to change your response toward it. This will not stop others from expecting to receive from you but can erect some well-needed borders and help in your overall well-being. Ask God to guide you in your response, especially in areas where your answer should be "no" or "not at this time," etc. Pick your involvement with scenarios that could benefit from your strengths but could easily place you in the same state of the excessive and harmful output you may be accustomed to.

Suppose you must lend your involvement to a particular undertaking because it is unavoidable (i.e., family/friend emergency, etc.). In that case, you need to be aware of things you can do. Learn effective delegation. Delegation is simply empowering someone else to take on specific responsibilities. When there is a fear of delegation, it is usually a sign of hesitation to trust or, worse, an inability to trust others with something important to you. This inability may have started with hurt. People hurt people. You have hurt people whether you were aware or not. When you have been injured, mistrust is a protective Band-Aid. It may help temporarily, but it does not support the underlying wound to heal correctly if it stays on indefinitely.

> At some point, God, in His wisdom and sovereignty, will require you to trust other people enough to delegate.
> You won't be able to trust everyone, but you will need to trust someone!

You cannot delegate everything. Certain things may need a level of responsibility that may not be present in those around you. However, there is almost always a way to delegate something out. You were not meant to carry it all alone.

Ask God to lead you in how delegation should be accomplished and to whom as this will involve trusting others to officiate in your stead. Ask God for the ability to trust in areas that have been bruised, broken, or mishandled. Keep your ear to the voice of God's direction and trust Him by following through on your borders and boundaries.

My Office Hours Are...

Learn time-management tips, including scheduling time for you to be alone and unwind. Set up effective boundaries and barriers that will allow you to slow down and be restored.

Realize the outward look of strength that you exude. Sometimes others are unaware of how much you carry as you make it look easy. Others may be aware, but their expectations *of* you may outweigh their concern *for* you. Learn to whom you can express your hurt and vulnerabilities; God has not intended that you hurt alone. However, you cannot be vulnerable to everyone! Even close friends and family can shatter trust. But God supplies our need for trusted individuals who, in conjunction with Him, help restore us from the bleeding episodes.

Prayer

Father God, thank You for being my Shepherd. You comfort my spirit and soul beyond natural ability. As You teach me, I learn to trust You when I hurt. Help me lean on You while You restore the places where I have been wounded and bruised. Help me manage the expectations others place on me while I'm hurting. Even when I'm injured, I thank You for letting me know I don't have to stay damaged. As I look to You, restore me and heal every wounded place. In Jesus's name, I pray. Amen.

Wisdom Nugget

I will trust and lean on the Lord when hurting. I will not resist the comfort or the therapeutic hand of the Lord when I am bruised or injured. I recognize the need to manage expectations from others as I heal so that I can continue to be in the position to bring comfort to others as I have been comforted.

My Declaration

Because of God's grace and love, I do not stay in a place of bleeding. I choose to be healed and get better and not bitter.

PROPHETIC LETTER:

I Prepare You to Be Ready

Beloved,

I am Elohim, the supreme God who has created all things. Do not be concerned about how your purpose fits where you are now. If I have prepared a place for you in heaven, do you not believe I have also prepared a place for you on the earth. If I have prepared where a wildflower will sprout, do not you think I also have plans for where to plant you? I am preparing you inside out and not outside in. Your heart is the centerpiece for My purposes in you. As I prepare and mold you from the heart, My handprint will be apparent to those I have assigned to you. My preparation is required, so you will be prepared for where I lead you. My assignments await you, and you will be prepared for them. When you question My hand or My leading, just know I have already gone before you. I am already in the place for which I am preparing for you.

Don't resist My preparation. It will not always be easy for you. You will feel the urge to resist because it will always push you out of the comfort you established for yourself. I will supply My servants to surround you and encourage you to push. You must push in order to prepare. Take pleasure in My promises during times of preparation. For you will be My mouthpiece. You will be My hands and feet. Stay steady in My Word; it will sustain you for the opposition that has been designed to resist you from reaching the prepared place. Take comfort in My mercy and grace that will be your sufficiency with every step. I am the one who prepares you. Therefore, you will be prepared and meet for My use.

CHAPTER 8:

I Manage Me

The LORD God took the man and put him in the
Garden of Eden to work it and take care of it.
—Genesis 2:15 (ESV)

God Created and Directed Us, but God Does Not Manage Us!

We are all familiar with the term "manager." The first image most people have is the person on their job who surveys their activities, performance, goals, etc. This person has quite a bit of input on your raise or bonus at the end of the year. Maybe you are a manager who manages others and, therefore, you are considered the authority over those subordinate to you. However, you still most likely have a manager over you as well. When we encounter people at a business who provide a service to us at a standard significantly above or below expectations, we may first ask, "Who is your manager?" Why? Because we are hoping once the manager is aware of the situation, they will take the appropriate action to either support or correct the problem and or actions of the person providing us service. We understand that a company must have proper management or authority structure, or else chaos and ultimate demise will occur.

The same system operates in almost everything that exists. Households must be managed. Finances must be managed. Relationships must be managed. The list can go on to include school, weight, hair, time, thoughts, etc. Everything must be handled or controlled in some way. Have you ever thought about who manages you? Not you as the employee, the mother, the father, the boss, etc. But *you*, the person, and the totality of all that encompasses who you are. If you think God manages you, it is an incorrect response. God does not manage you. God is your creator, and He is your ultimate source for anything you may need or desire.

> God provides us with everything necessary to regulate the resources we are to control, handle, master, or influence.

Scripture reveals "His divine power has granted to us all things that pertain to life and godliness, through the knowledge of him who called us to his own glory and excellence" (2 Peter 1:3, ESV). God will direct, guide, instruct, reward, and provide anything we may need to fulfill the godly call and purpose that He has placed within us. However, God has never been responsible for managing us. God has never managed anyone; he created us to be the managers! Even the first Adam was placed here to contain or be in charge of the resources given to him. "Then the LORD God took the man and put him in the garden of Eden to tend and keep it" (Genesis 2:15, NKJV). God made the garden, but the garden needed to be managed. God created man, but man needs to be managed.

God made me aware years ago that everything needed to be managed. I was studying the scripture Deuteronomy 29:29

(ESV), which states: "The secret things belong to God, but that which He reveals belongs unto the children of man." God spoke and told me anything that "belongs" to us must be managed! Even revelation. Just because revelation is given to us does not mean anything. How we tend to it and keep it determines our success in what God reveals to us. Anything and anyone unmanaged or poorly managed will become chaotic. God made the earth and everything in it, but he placed us here to sustain it. How we handle ourselves is critical. The parts of ourselves that we don't correctly manage will turn disorderly.

Other people will follow how well or poorly you manage yourself. If you tend to yourself well, others will perceive how they should treat you based on how you treat yourself. Similarly, if you tend to yourself poorly, people will, in turn, either mistreat you or leave. As your manager, you decide what has rightful access to you and when access should be denied. People do not remain around what they perceive as chaotic. As you are your own manager, high levels of access to you should not be allowed if treatment is substandard. We must prepare and maintain *how* to manage ourselves and the access others have to us. It should not just happen on its own. Just because you have lived with yourself daily does not mean you know yourself well enough to manage yourself. Management takes preparation. This chapter is about preparing you to manage yourself more efficiently.

There are certain parts of you that only you can regulate or master. This is a job you are unable to give away. Only you can do it. No matter how strong you manage situations or others, the structure eventually falls apart if you cannot control yourself well. I know you want to develop the leader that is inside of you. But what about the person behind the leader? The first person you must be able to lead is you.

Recognize Unmanaged or Mismanaged Areas

One word can sum up what unmanaged or mismanaged areas in our lives look like—disorder! Unmanaged rooms are those areas that are cluttered from lack of organization. Dirty rooms are usually due to a lack of discipline in keeping them clean. Even clean rooms that are not used much will show signs that they have not been attended to if they are not managed. You may have cleaned and unused room two months ago, but it will still gather dust, spider webs, and other signs that people are not present there if it is not used. Don't forget those rooms within our thinking that just need an overhaul. Those ways of thinking where we have gotten so comfortable that we are no longer challenged to grow. Open yourself to explore the "rooms" inside you that others see and express as needing management. Maybe it is a lack of follow-through. This is a central unmanaged area for a lot of people. You may be great at starting something, but it's the completion of something that establishes it. Do you return calls, emails, or messages? Did you finish reading that book or performing that task or assignment? Lack of follow-through and execution is noticeable, both being costly unmanaged areas for many. Maybe financial management is needed. Regardless of the amount of money, unmanaged or mismanaged money will ultimately cost you! If we are not used to managing ourselves financially, the answer to many of our issues may not be the need to make more but rather to manage more.

What Does Excellent Self-Management Look Like?

When we manage ourselves well, we present a solid image that will be an inside-out success. What do I mean by "inside-out success"? Simply put: how you look on the outside should reflect how you look inside. You may know of people who present very well on the outside but not doing so well on the inside. We all face issues and challenges in life; I am not stating we have to have everything together at all times. Some challenges can take the most composed person out of character. I'm talking about those who present as if they can lead you to a higher level in the desired area of your life. Still, they need help in multiple places (financially, emotionally, physiologically, etc.). You cannot consistently find what you need from them as things shift to them needing to pull from you because of multiple unmanaged conditions in their lives. A well-managed person can be a supply to those they are called to without spinning the responsibility back on the person to take care of them.

It's okay that we don't have it all together. No one does! But don't portray the ability that you are ready to supply what you are not prepared to deliver. When Jesus came to the fig tree expecting figs, the leaves told a different story, even though it was not the time for figs. The fact that leaves were on the tree was an indication that it would supply what it was purposed to produce. The fig tree was purposed to provide figs. But all it had was an appearance that it was making what it was purposed to produce.

This chapter is about establishing a management plan to help sustain you authentically in your purpose. You can be authentic and unmanaged at the same time. However, it is not as effective as being authentic and well-managed.

Why is it essential to establish and maintain a self-management plan? Because we tend to be apathetic in the unmanaged areas of our lives. Therefore, we are susceptible to disorder in some areas of our lives unless we have reason to bring them to order. A plan can help us distinguish those areas in need and motivate us to bring order to those areas. A plan brings order and motivation.

The "I Manage Me" Plan

We must receive and agree with who God made us. One of the most significant issues I have found among God's people is that we don't know or believe who God has called us. This must be the first place we start when formulating our plan.

> You are the one that must tell yourself who you are based on what God says and has placed in you, even if you do not yet see the most significant degree of it.

There is great power when we agree with what God has spoken about us! I think most of us know about the power of agreement. The principle of agreement is fundamental to God. He set up man's earth dominion centered on this truth. This principle works so well; the Bible says God came down to the earth to disrupt the people's agreement to build the tower of Babel—because they succeeded within the principle of this unity. "Agreement" means "the absence of incompatibility and disharmony." It is the consistency and harmony between two or more things. When we fall out of agreement with something, we are on the opposing side of it. God wants us in accord with His Word and His plan. We must be in so much agreement with the Word of God regarding us that there is no room for doubt, incompatibility, or disharmony. Instead, we walk in synchronization and alignment with what God has placed inside us in complete acceptance.

Our agreement with His word causes a legal connection in the spirit with what God has spoken. As we come into a legal binding with the word of God, we will have victory in everything ordained by the terms of God, as the word of God cannot return to Him without completing its assignment.

This may take a while for some. It's okay. Just keep walking in harmony with God and associating with the people God has placed in your path to provide wisdom, counsel, and mentorship. You will not get there alone. You will always need the people God sends to you to help complete your purpose picture.

> Accepting responsibility for managing what God has placed in you is crucial in the preparatory phase of your purpose journey. It is impossible to handle yourself in those areas for which you have not taken some responsibility.

In creating the "I Manage Me" plan, we will adjust our perspective and take the responsibility to walk in purpose while sustaining ourselves physically, emotionally, and spiritually.

Section I

MANAGING YOUR PERCEPTIONS

You must bring clarity to what you see as your God-given purpose.

1. What are your primary gifts from God?

   _____

   _____

   _____

   _____

2. What is your God-given purpose? Describe your sense of why you are here. (If you are still in the discovery phase, then record this as your answer, but dig deep and state what you feel is your primary purpose from God.)

   _____

   _____

   _____

   _____

3. What do you find that you supply to others? What do others place a demand on you for?

   _____

   _____

   _____

   _____

   _____

4. Write the vision of your God-purpose using questions 1–3. Write a cohesive statement of who you are and what you supply to form a cohesive picture of your purpose.

_____

_____

_____

_____

_____

_____

ACCEPTING WHAT OTHERS SEE IN YOU HELPS YOU RECEIVE WHAT GOD PLACED IN YOU

5. Write a list of statements you hear the most from others about you. (This may require some time and thought but is worth the time commitment). Remember to interpret the negative statements as what is seen and not necessarily what is said.

_____

_____

_____

_____

_____

_____

_____

_____

6. How do the statements in question 5 confirm or clarify your purpose as described in question 4?

_____

_____

_____

_____

_____

MANAGING FALSE PERSPECTIVES

It would help if you made your purpose your confession. Speak *life* to who God says you are. Don't wait for others to declare this over you. You must exemplify what God has called you.

7. Find scripture(s) that speak to your God-given purpose and write them here.

_____

_____

_____

_____

_____

_____

_____

8. Meditate on the above scriptures daily (protect and nurture what God has spoken over you). Write down any consistent thoughts that do not agree with your answers to questions 1–5.

_____

_____

_____

_____

9. Using what you have learned about yourself in questions 1–8, write your declaration of the new perspective you have of yourself regarding your purpose. Make the declaration short so that you can confess it daily, especially when you recognize a return to old perceptions of yourself.

_____

_____

_____

_____

_____

_____

_____

_____

_____

_____

Section 2

ACHIEVING EMOTIONAL
RELEASE/BALANCE

10. Where or what is my place(s) of release? Name the places, times, or scenarios where you have felt the most freedom to release your emotions? *(Healthy releasing of tears, worship, venting, screaming, etc.)*

_____

_____

_____

_____

_____

_____

_____

_____

_____

_____

_____

_____

11. Your willingness to release your tears is crucial. Chose to release and submit every tear needed to sustain you in a good place of well-being. Write a declaration for yourself that you can read and repeat daily. *Example: I have the courage to release the things I fear to remember or recount. I do not hold in emotional baggage as I realize the harm it inflicts. I recognize my need to release and give myself permission to release as often as needed.*

_____

_____

_____

_____

_____

_____

_____

_____

_____

_____

_____

_____

_____

_____

_____

Section 3

MANAGING THE WEIGHT OF OTHERS

12. Write down the weight of others that is obligatory and, therefore, must be carried (i.e., children, aging parents, job, etc.) Once written, write down a plan that will help you balance these obligations.

_____

_____

_____

_____

_____

_____

_____

_____

_____

_____

_____

_____

_____

_____

_____

_____

_____

13. List those extra activities and weights (needs from others outside of your required daily responsibilities). Recognize when these extra weights bring you too close to your defined capacity at any given time. How will you recognize what weights you must remove to keep you from exceeding your defined self-capacity?

_____

_____

_____

_____

_____

_____

_____

_____

_____

_____

_____

_____

_____

_____

_____

RECOGNIZING THE CONDITION
OF YOUR INNER MAN

14. Write down your plan to strengthen the condition of your spirit, or inner man. (Daily activities like prayer, reading God's Word, etc.)

_____

_____

_____

_____

_____

_____

_____

_____

_____

_____

_____

_____

_____

_____

_____

_____

_____

Section 4

MANAGING YOUR PRODUCTION AND ACCESSIBILITY

Setting realistic boundaries and borders

15. Let's set and keep realistic borders that safeguard your well-being. Think of the two areas needing borders (limits you set on yourself to guard your health, well-being, or stability). These are areas you have abused and need the management that well-established borders should supply (time, relationships, finances, weight, etc.).

_____

_____

_____

_____

_____

_____

_____

_____

_____

_____

_____

_____

16. Let's set boundaries that protect your accessibility from potential abuse from others. Think of the two areas needing boundaries (limits that you set to guard yourself against the abuse from others). These are areas that others have abused regarding you (resources, time, misuse of your compassion, etc.). Also, include how you will communicate your boundaries to others. You cannot enact consequences for a boundary you fail to define and express.

_____

_____

_____

_____

_____

_____

_____

_____

_____

_____

_____

_____

_____

_____

_____

Identifying self-sabotage

17. Recall and record examples of times that you have broken the borders that you set for yourself. Then write what you need to put in place to keep you from breaking those borders.

_____

_____

_____

_____

_____

_____

_____

_____

_____

_____

_____

_____

_____

_____

_____

_____

Section 5

YOUR SOURCES OF STRENGTH

18. Identify the human sources of strength that God sent to you and record why they reflect God's help.

_____

_____

_____

_____

_____

_____

_____

19. Record how you will receive and learn from God's sources sent to you.

_____

_____

_____

_____

_____

_____

_____

_____

Section 6

RECOGNIZING SABOTAGE

Rejection, intimidation, and offense are inevitable when you do things successfully. How will you deal with these sabotaging forces?

20. What are the major forces of sabotage you experience from others?

_____

_____

_____

_____

_____

_____

21. What do you recognize as the major forces of self-sabotage in your life?

_____

_____

_____

_____

_____

_____

_____

22. What is your strategy for dealing with the main saboteurs in your life?

_____

_____

_____

_____

_____

_____

Section 7

MANAGING THE MISMANAGED AREAS WITHIN YOURSELF

23. Based on your experience, what red flags do you exhibit (i.e., yelling, short temper, crying spells, etc.) when your capacity to produce has been exceeded?

_____

_____

_____

_____

_____

_____

_____

24. What key area can you identify that needs to be better managed in your life? These are the areas that display disorder and, therefore, need better management. Try to deal with the most pressing area(s) of need.

_____

_____

_____

_____

_____

_____

_____

_____

_____

_____

_____

_____

_____

_____

_____

Use your responses above to fill out your "I Manage Me" plan.

Write Out Your
"I Manage Me" Plan

I, (Name)_____**, am purposed by God to**
(use question 1–4 to help you discover your primary purpose)

_____

_____

_____

_____

_____

_____

_____

according to Scripture text (use question 7)

_____

_____

_____

_____

_____

_____

_____

_____

_____

I recognize how I service others are in the areas of (use questions 3 and 6)

_____

_____

_____

_____

_____

_____

_____

_____

_____

I read my purpose declaration daily (use question 9)

_____

_____

_____

_____

_____

_____

_____

I reject other perspectives of myself that go against my God-given purpose.

I understand I must help manage my emotional well-being. I choose to allow myself to release myself emotionally. (Use Question 11 to write down where you feel the most freedom to release. Make the regular opportunity to engage in the activities that you record.)

_____

_____

_____

_____

_____

_____

I recognize I must manage myself within the capacity created for me. Therefore, I will not allow constant extra weight beyond that capacity. Here are my required obligations (use question 12).

_____

_____

_____

_____

_____

_____

Here are the responsibilities I chose to take on outside my required daily activities. I allow myself to reduce or eliminate the following duties at this time. (Use Question 13 to help detail your responsibilities.)

_____

_____

_____

_____

_____

_____

I strengthened my inner man daily through prayer, Scripture, and meditation. I will fast as God leads me.

Based on the need to manage my output, I have set the following borders (areas that safeguard my well-being), and I will abide by my current borders. (Use Question 15 to detail your borders.)

_____

_____

_____

_____

_____

_____

_____

I set the following well-defined boundaries based on the need to manage my access. I will make others aware of my limitations and enact consequences when boundaries are breached. (Use question 16 to detail your boundaries.)

_____

_____

_____

_____

_____

_____

_____

_____

I recognize and lean on the people God sent to aid me in my life and purpose. (Use questions 18 and 19 to list them and write how you will receive from them.)

_____

_____

_____

_____

_____

_____

_____

I understand that my response to the opposition against my purpose must be managed well. Here are my strategies when faced with a challenging opponent. (Use questions 20–22 to help formulate a plan against the force(s) that resist you the most.)

_____

_____

_____

_____

_____

_____

_____

_____

_____

_____

_____

_____

_____

_____

_____

I thank God for creating me to be who I am. I also realize He has given me the resources to help steward my purpose in the best way to be a blessing to others. I chose to manage better my mismanaged areas to be wholly practical in my purpose. These are the areas I commit to working better within the next six months. (Use questions 23–24 to help you identify the areas [for example, financial management, weight management, etc.]. Commit to outlining what you will use to help you better manage these areas and the time frame the improvement will take you.)

_____

_____

_____

_____

_____

_____

_____

_____

_____

_____

_____

_____

_____

_____

EPILOGUE

This book was a journey for me, as I was instructed to release some critical areas of God's wisdom supplied to me over the years. After reading this book and completing the management plan, you have journeyed deeper into the strong person you are and recognized the part you play in walking victoriously in your purpose. You have strengthened your understanding of why you are here and how your purpose plays within God's great purpose for humanity. You have learned how to manage the incredible strength God has graced you to operate within your personal life and the kingdom of God. Your strength was not an afterthought with God. You were ordained for the time you now live in. You are given assignments by God that will bring meaning to you as you supply others with the elements they need to discover and develop the purpose that God has given them. As you carry out each assignment, challenge yourself to draw on the wisdom of God. He has chosen you to be an inspiration in a world where everyone has not been established with the responsibility of your strength.

You are a leader, an influencer, and a survivor. But you cannot obtain all your goals alone. You need the strength that comes from others. You need the input others can provide. You now receive the help representing our heavenly Father to aid and comfort you. You prioritize your emotional well-being. As you go forward, you will not only understand yourself to a greater degree, but you will better handle yourself within each area of your life. You can place more meaning in the roles people have within your life and why they were allowed to play those roles.

Use your "I Manage Me" plan to help you formulate strategies that improve those areas needing better management; redirect and resist sabotage and provide the necessary motivation to encourage you to keep moving in your purpose journey.

I look forward to future endeavors that will help develop leaders who leverage their areas of influence. I pray you will find strength, encouragement, and the assurance needed to sustain yourself. You are the *strong* person behind a *strong* purpose!

NOTES

"The Strong One": Godly Wisdom for the Person Behind the Purpose

ABOUT THE AUTHOR

Debra Byas is an associate pastor, the founder and the leader of an international women's ministry, business owner, and author. Pastor Debra is passionate about mentoring women to strategize their lives for the intentional and persistent pursuit of their God-given purpose. With a foundation built in lifelong prayer coupled with twenty-five years as a Bible scholar and teacher, Debra is devoted to hearing and obeying the voice of God as she ministers to women of all ages and denominations. She has over fifteen years of speaking at churches, women's conferences, and special events.

Debra learned the value of mentorship early as it was absent from her early-adult life. She desperately longed for someone who would genuinely help her realize and develop her God-given purpose. She combed through books, television, and other media but greatly missed the personal presence of leaders who would unselfishly walk her through what she felt God placed inside her. This absence inspired her to develop, cultivate, and mentor younger women to pursue and be purposely excellent in their gifts and calling.

Pastor Debra's mission is to develop followers into purposely excellent leaders in their area(s) of influence. Her goal is to assist them in their quest to fulfill God's intent for their lives.

Debra and her husband, Pastor Carl Byas, live in Wilmington, North Carolina. They have four young adults and one grandson.

**To learn more about Pastor Debra
or how to book her for speaking,
master classes, or mentoring programs,
visit Debrabyas.com.**

"The Strong One": Godly Wisdom for the Person Behind the Purpose

ENDNOTES

1   Lexico.com, s.v. "authentic," accessed June 9, 2022, www.lexico.com/en/definition/authentic.

2   Wiktionary, s.v. "conform," last edited on 1 June 2022, www.en.wiktionary.org/wiki/conform.

3   *Merriam-Webster.com Dictionary*, s.v. "confirm," accessed June 9, 2022, www.merriam-webster.com/dictionary/confirm.

4   *Merriam-Webster.com Dictionary*, s.v. "complex," accessed June 9, 2022, https://www.merriam-webster.com/dictionary/complex.

5   Lexico.com, s.v. "boundary," accessed June 9, 2022, www.lexico.com/en/definition/ boundary.

6   *Merriam-Webster.com Dictionary*, s.v. "border," accessed June 9, 2022, https://www.merriam-webster.com/dictionary/border.

7   *Merriam-Webster.com Dictionary*, s.v. "reject," accessed June 9, 2022, https://www.merriam-webster.com/dictionary/reject.

8   *Merriam-Webster.com Dictionary*, s.v. "intimidate," accessed June 9, 2022, https://www.merriam-webster.com/dictionary/intimidate.

9   *Merriam-Webster.com Dictionary*, s.v. "offense," accessed June 9, 2022, https://www.merriam-webster.com/dictionary/offense.

CPSIA information can be obtained
at www.ICGtesting.com
Printed in the USA
LVHW051123120723
751664LV00005B/204